# TEACHER'S PET PUBLICATIONS

LITPLAN TEACHER PACK
for
The Slave Dancer
based on the book by
Paula Fox

Written by
Janine H. Sherman

© 1996 Teacher's Pet Publications
All Rights Reserved

This **LitPlan** for Paula Fox's
The Slave Dancer
has been brought to you by Teacher's Pet Publications, Inc.

Copyright Teacher's Pet Publications 1996
11504 Hammock Point
Berlin MD 21811

Only the student materials in this unit plan (such as worksheets,
study questions, and tests) may be reproduced multiple times
for use in the purchaser's classroom.

For any additional copyright questions,
contact Teacher's Pet Publications.

www.tpet.com

TABLE OF CONTENTS - *Slave Dancer*

Introduction	5
Unit Objectives	8
Reading Assignment Sheet	9
Unit Outline	10
Study Questions (Short Answer)	13
Quiz/Study Questions (Multiple Choice)	26
Pre-reading Vocabulary Worksheets	49
Lesson One (Introductory Lesson)	67
Nonfiction Assignment Sheet	70
Oral Reading Evaluation Form	85
Writing Assignment 1	69
Writing Assignment 2	87
Writing Assignment 3	93
Writing Evaluation Form	78
Project	89
Vocabulary Review Activities	101
Extra Writing Assignments/Discussion ?s	95
Unit Review Activities	103
Unit Tests	107
Unit Resource Materials	149
Vocabulary Resource Materials	165

A FEW NOTES ABOUT THE AUTHOR
Paula Fox

FOX, Paula (1923-   ). Paula Fox was born in New York, New York. Her father was a writer, and he and her mother moved around a lot. Paula did not always live with them. She spent her early years living with a Congregational minister and his aged mother, in a big Victorian house that overlooked New York's Hudson River. The minister, a former newspaperman himself, often read to her from his own work. Their house was filled with books which Paula began reading at the tender age of five. She's been reading ever since. It seems to her that it's the essential work of the writer.

She left the minister's house when she was six years old to live with her parents in California and then on a sugar plantation in Cuba. In Cuba, she attended a one-room schoolhouse and became fluent in Spanish. Later, she was taken back to New York City. By the age of twelve, she had gone to nine schools. It was an unsettling childhood, one she is still trying to understand many years later through her writing. Each character in her books reflects her life's experiences, in ways she can't always explain. "I wasn't on a slave ship," she says, referring to Newbery Award Medal Winner, *The Slave Dancer (*1975). "I wasn't a boy who thought he shot a cat," referring to Newbery Award Honor Book, *The One-Eyed Cat (1982)*. "But those experiences are somehow rooted in my own sense of life, or how I see life, how I've experienced it."

When Paula Fox first got the idea for *The Slave Dancer*, she knew she had to do a lot of research to make the story come alive. She remembers someone at the library guiding her to a tremendous area of books on slavery. Her heart sank. She didn't know how to do research. But she learned. She forced herself to open the first book. Then everything became possible. She admits, "You have to pick a point. And it's not that you can find a beginning, because there is no beginning. From that first point, I went on. It's like crossing a stream on stepping stones. One step leads you to another." After a year of research, she threw the notes away when she started writing because they paralyzed her with information.

Paula Fox wishes kids would read instead of watch TV. She says, "When you begin to read, read everything. Reading helps you think about things, imagine what it feels like to be somebody else...even somebody you don't like!" She has written over thirteen books including *Monkey Island* (1991), *The King's Falcon* (1992), *Amzat and His Brothers*, and *Western Wind* (1993). She currently resides in Brooklyn, New York.

INTRODUCTION - *The Slave Dancer*

This unit has been designed to develop students' reading, writing, thinking, and language skills through exercises and activities related to *The Slave Dancer* by Paula Fox. It includes twenty lessons supported by extra resource materials plus a class project.

The **introductory lesson** introduces students to background information about places, people, and events mentioned throughout this novel. It also doubles as the first writing assignment for the unit. Following the introductory activity, students are given an explanation of how the activity relates to the book they are about to read. The next lesson following the transition, students are given the materials they will be using during the unit.

The **reading assignments** are approximately twenty pages each; some are a little shorter while others are a little longer. Students have approximately 15 minutes of Pre-reading work to do prior to each reading assignment. This Pre-reading work involves reviewing the study questions for the assignment and doing some vocabulary work for ten to twelve vocabulary words they will encounter in their reading.

The **study guide questions** are fact-based questions; students can find the answers to these questions right in the text. These questions come in two formats: short answer or multiple choice. The best use of these materials is probably to use the short answer version of the questions as study guides for students (since answers will be more complete), and to use the multiple choice version for occasional quizzes. It might be a good idea to make transparencies of your answer keys for the overhead projector.

The **vocabulary work** is intended to enrich students' vocabularies as well as to aid in the students' understanding of the book. Prior to each reading assignment, students will complete a two-part worksheet for approximately ten to twelve vocabulary words in the upcoming reading assignment. Part I focuses on students' use of general knowledge and contextual clues by giving the sentence in which the word appears in the text. Students are then to write down what they think the words mean based on the words' usage. Part II nails down the definitions of the words by giving students dictionary definitions of the words and having students match the words to the correct definitions based on the words' contextual usage. Students should then have an understanding of the words when they meet them in the text.

After each reading assignment, students will go back and formulate answers for the study guide questions. Discussion of these questions serves as a **review** of the most important events and ideas presented in the reading assignments.

After students complete extra discussion questions, there is a **vocabulary review** lesson which pulls together all of the fragmented vocabulary lists for the reading assignments and gives students a review of all of the words they have studied.

Following the reading of the book, two lessons are devoted to the **extra discussion questions/writing assignments/activities**. These questions focus on interpretation, critical analysis and personal response, employing a variety of thinking skills and adding to the students' understanding of the novel. These questions are done as a **group activity**. Using the information they have acquired so far through individual work and class discussions, students get together to further examine the text and to brainstorm ideas relating to the themes of the novel.

The group activity is followed by a **reports and discussion/ activity** session in which the groups share their ideas about the book with the entire class; thus, the entire class gets exposed to many different ideas regarding the themes and events of the book.

There are three **writing assignments** in this unit, each with the purpose of informing, persuading, or having students express personal opinions. The first assignment is to inform: students write a composition about one of the background topics assigned in Lesson One. The second assignment gives students the chance to persuade: students pretend they live in the 1840's and are violently opposed to all aspects of slave trading. They are to convince slaveowners to stop promoting this practice. The third assignment is to give students the opportunity to express personal ideas: students will share how music influences and colors their lives.

The **nonfiction reading assignment** is tied in with Writing Assignment 1 and the introductory lesson. Students are required to read a piece of nonfiction related in some way to *The Slave Dancer*. In this case, the topics are assigned in Lesson One. After reading their nonfiction pieces, students will fill out a worksheet on which they answer questions regarding facts, interpretation, criticism, and personal opinions. During one class period, students make **oral presentations** about the nonfiction pieces they have read. This not only exposes all students to a wealth of information, it also gives students the opportunity to practice **public speaking**.

There is an optional **class project** (Multicultural Awareness) through which students will gain an appreciation of many cultures and the challenges of multicultural equality. They also will have the opportunity to take part in helping to do something to foster this ideal in their community.

The **review lesson** pulls together all of the aspects of the unit. The teacher is given four or five choices of activities or games to use which all serve the same basic function of reviewing all of the information presented in the unit.

The **unit test** comes in two formats: all multiple choice-matching-true/false or with a mixture of matching, short answer, and composition. As a convenience, two different tests for each format have been included.

There are additional **support materials** included with this unit. The **resource sections** include suggestions for an in-class library, crossword and word search puzzles related to the novel, and extra vocabulary worksheets. There is a list of **bulletin board ideas** which gives the teacher suggestions for bulletin boards to go along with this unit. In addition, there is a list of **extra class activities** the teacher could choose from to enhance the unit or as a substitution for an exercise the teacher might feel is inappropriate for his/her class. **Answer keys** are located directly after the **reproducible student materials** throughout the unit. The student materials may be reproduced for use in the teacher's classroom without infringement of copyrights. No other portion of this unit may be reproduced without the written consent of Teacher's Pet Publications, Inc.

UNIT OBJECTIVES - *The Slave Dancer*

1. Through reading Paula Fox's *The Slave Dancer,* students will gain an understanding of the effects of cruelty and the vicious cycle it can create.

2. Students will be exposed to gross racial injustice portrayed through the horrors of slavery.

3. Students will do background research to become familiar with relevant geographical locales and the history of slave trade.

4. Students will become familiar with and able to identify ship terminology.

5. Students will demonstrate their understanding of the text on four levels: factual, interpretive, critical and personal.

6. Students will gain appreciation for and demonstrate proficiency in identifying and using figurative language.

7. Students will be given the opportunity to practice reading aloud and silently to improve their skills in each area.

8. Students will answer questions to demonstrate their knowledge and understanding of the main events and characters in *The Slave Dancer* as they relate to the author's theme development.

9. Students will enrich their vocabularies and improve their understanding of the novel through the vocabulary lessons prepared for use in conjunction with the novel.

10. The writing assignments in this unit are geared to several purposes:
    a. To have students demonstrate their abilities to inform, to persuade, or to express their own personal ideas
        Note: Students will demonstrate ability to write effectively to <u>inform</u> by developing and organizing facts to convey information. Students will demonstrate the ability to write effectively to <u>persuade</u> by selecting and organizing relevant information, establishing an argumentative purpose, and by designing an appropriate strategy for an identified audience. Students will demonstrate the ability to write effectively to <u>express personal ideas</u> by selecting a form and its appropriate elements.
    b. To check the students' reading comprehension
    c. To make students think about the ideas presented by the novel
    d. To encourage logical thinking

READING ASSIGNMENT SHEET - *The Slave Dancer*

Date to be Assigned	Chapters (pages)	Completion Date
	History; The Errand (vii-11)	
	The Moonlight (12-34)	
	The Shrouds (35-48)	
	The Bight of Benin (49-68)	
	Nicholas Spark Walks On Water (69-89)	
	The Spaniard (90-112)	
	Ben Stout's Mistake (113-132)	
	The Old Man; Home and After (133-152)	

UNIT OUTLINE - *The Slave Dancer*

1 Library Writing Assignment #1	2 Introduction	3 PVR History; The Errand	4 Study? History; The Errand PVR The Moonlight	5 Study? The Moonlight PVR The Shrouds
6 Study? The Shrouds Characterization	7 PVR The Bight of Benin Writing Conference	8 Study ? The Bight of Benin PV Nicholas Spark Walks On Water	9 Group Activity Figurative Language	10 Read Nicholas Spark Walks On Water Oral Reading Evaluation
11 Study? Nicholas Spark Walks On Water PVR The Spaniard Writing Ass't. 2	12 Study ? The Spaniard PVR Ben Stout's Mistake	13 Study ? Ben Stout's Mistake PV The Old Man; Home and After	14 Read The Old Man; Home and After	15 Writing Assignment #3
16 Extra Discussion Questions	17 Extra Discussion Questions/ Activities	18 Vocabulary Review	19 Review	20 Test
21 Project	22	23	24	25

Key: P=Preview Study Questions   V= Vocabulary Work   R= Read

STUDY GUIDE QUESTIONS

SHORT ANSWER STUDY GUIDE QUESTIONS - *The Slave Dancer*

History; The Errand
1. What type of disaster occurs to The Moonlight according to History?
2. How does Jessie's mother support her family?
3. Betty, Jessie's sister, is bothered by what weather condition in New Orleans?
4. What does Jessie imagine the fog is?
5. Give the setting for this chapter in the novel.
6. Where had Jessie been earlier that day that was forbidden to him?
7. Why doesn't Jessie care for Aunt Agatha?
8. How and when did Jessie's father die?
9. Where and why does Jessie's mother send him on an errand?
10. In what manner does Aunt Agatha treat Jessie when he comes for the candles?
11. What does Jessie remember while walking by the walled gardens of the rich families?
12. On the way home, Jessie envisions himself a fine rich man. What disrupts his daydream?
13. What did Jessie think about as he stared at the black water the raft was travelling on?
14. Where and when had Jessie seen one of his kidnappers before?

The Moonlight
1. Where do Jessie's captors deposit him?
2. Which of Jessie's five senses was assaulted upon falling on the deck?
3. When Jessie expresses concern over his mother worrying, what does Purvis tell him?
4. Describe Benjamin Stout.
5. Describe Captain Cawthorne.
6. How does the Captain hurt Jessie and why?
7. Where is the ship bound and for what purpose?
8. What does the Captain exchange the slaves for in Africa?
9. Why was Jessie needed?
10. In what does Jessie sleep?
11. Why do the British try to block the other slave traders?
12. What does Ben Stout say they're a dead ship without?
13. Hunting and killing of what rodent was a daily ship routine?
14. Describe Purvis.

The Shrouds
1. Other than the British, who else makes slave running hazardous?
2. What jobs filled up Jessie's days on the ship?
3. Jessie used to think the sea was always blue. What colors does he see now?
4. When did Jessie become most fearful?
5. Even though Ben Stout treats Jessie well, who does Jessie prefer?
6. What changes occurred on the ship once it had becalmed?

Short Answer Study Questions *Slave Dancer* Page 2

The Shrouds continued
7. While sleeping on the deck, what did Jessie see one night?
8. Who was wrongfully accused and punished by the Captain for stealing the egg?
9. When Jessie questioned Purvis about why he didn't turn in the real culprit, Stout, how did Purvis respond?

The Bight of Benin
1. How do slaving ships employ different flags to their advantage?
2. What does Purvis ask Jessie to do that he has not done since he'd been on the ship?
3. When the crew sights land, what disturbing view was seen?
4. What does the fire remind Jessie of?
5. When does the crew get to go on land?
6. Why is it necessary for Jessie to play his fife for the slaves?
7. Upon seeing land, how does Jessie's mood change?
8. Jessie's comment about the kidnapping of the slaves causes Purvis to react in what way?
9. What is Jessie ordered to do with the rum he was told to fetch?
10. How and when were the slaves loaded on the ship?
11. How long was *The Moonlight* at the Bight of Benin?
12. For what reason is Jessie smacked by Ned?
13. How many slaves has the crew loaded on *The Moonlight?*

Nicholas Spark Walks On Water
1. For what reason did *The Moonlight* sail away from Wydah at night?
2. Name the African tribe the blacks loaded on the ship are part of.
3. Which crew member admits to the evilness of slave trading?
4. Name the three crew members seemingly untouched by the blacks suffering.
5. Explain Jessie's reaction to seeing the naked blacks herded onto the deck to be made to dance.
6. If the slaves will not dance, what happens to them?
7. How often must Jessie 'dance' the slaves?
8. Tell the fate of the screaming black woman.
9. What realization does Jessie have that causes him to defy his orders?
10. What role did Stout play in the 'mad' black woman's fate according to Purvis?
11. How is Jessie able to temporarily escape the horrors of the ship?
12. When Jessie notices the black boy his age watching him, what does he do?
13. Which crew member did the Captain punish for shooting a slave?
14. Jessie questions Ned about his illness. What is his reply?

Short Answer Study Questions *Slave Dancer* Page 3

The Spaniard
1. Which crew member replaces the First Mate?
2. How does Jessie respond to Stout's questioning about the morale of the crew?
3. How does Purvis characterize Stout to Jessie?
4. Where does Stout place Jessie's flute and what must Jessie do to retrieve it?
5. In what manner does Purvis try to cheer up Jessie?
6. What is the strange stirring Jessie sees in the water over the rail.
7. What is Sharkey's opinion about the slaves' shackles?
8. Describe the Spaniard and his slave.
9. Where does Jessie vow never to visit again if he ever makes it home?

Ben Stout's Mistake
1. What chore was Jessie sent to the Captain's quarters to complete?
2. How does the Captain reward Jessie for not knowing what is in the chest?
3. What does the Captain point out to the Spaniard who comments, "A miracle!"
4. What is in the chest and for what purpose?
5. After the slaves are dressed, now what must they do?
6. Why is the festivity halted?
7. What revelation causes the Captain to order the slaves overboard?
8. What act of nature takes over at this point?
9. How did Jessie and the black boy avoid further danger?
10. After the boys awaken and Jessie climbs out to the deck, what does he see?
11. When Jessie goes back to the hold, he and the black boy wait out the storm. What do they do next?
12. What does Jessie think kept him going when he could only dogpawing?

The Old Man
1. Name the first living thing the boys see upon reaching the shore in Mississippi.
2. What words does Jessie say to himself while dog pawing from the ship to the shore?
3. Daniel tells Jessie what information about the bodies from the ship?
4. How did Jessie and Daniel spend their time with Daniel?
5. Where does Ras go?
6. On their last day together, what piece of the ship did Ras and Jessie find on the beach?
7. What does Jessie promise Daniel before he leaves?

Short Answer Study Questions *Slave Dancer* Page 4

<u>Home and After</u>
1. What did Jessie fear the most on his journey home?
2. How many days did Jessie's trip home take?
3. How does Jessie's mother handle his absence and return?
4. What type of vocation does Jessie learn?
5. What happened to Jessie after moving to Rhode Island?
6. How was Jessie affected musically by his experience?

STUDY GUIDE QUESTION ANSWERS - *The Slave Dancer*

<u>History ; The Errand</u>

1. What type of disaster occurs to *The Moonlight* according to History?
   According to History, *The Moonlight* shipwrecks in the Gulf of Mexico, June 3, 1840.

2. How does Jessie's mother support her family?
   Jessie's mother was a seamstress; making gowns for the rich ladies of New Orleans.

3. Betty, Jessie's sister, is bothered by what weather condition in New Orleans?
   The dampness causes Betty to cough, filling the room with barking sounds.

4. What does Jessie imagine the fog is?
   He imagines it is a kind of sweat thrown off by the Mississippi River as it goes out to sea.

5. Give the setting for this chapter in the novel.
   It takes place in New Orleans, Louisiana during late January of 1840.

6. Where had Jessie been earlier that day that was forbidden to him?
   He had spent an hour wandering about the slave market at the corner of St. Louis and Chartres Streets.

7. Why doesn't Jessie care for Aunt Agatha?
   He finds her very disagreeable, bossy, and critical. She insults him regularly.

8. How and when did Jessie's father die?
   He drowned nine years earlier in the Mississippi River while working to clear it of tree stumps and other hidden debris for steamboat passage.

9. Where and why does Jessie's mother send him on an errand?
   She needed more candles so that she can work longer into the night on her sewing.

10. In what manner does Aunt Agatha treat Jessie when he comes for the candles?
    She openly criticizes him and says his mother shouldn't sew at night anyhow. She thinks he should not play his flute to earn money, but needs to be apprenticed to learn a trade.

11. What does Jessie remember while walking by the walled gardens of the rich families?
    He recalls a slave woman watching him as he climbed the walls one day to peek in. She was summoned back to the house by someone calling the name 'Star'. He was fascinated by the name, and wondered what she thought of it.

12. On the way home, Jessie envisions himself a fine rich man. What disrupts his daydream?
    Two men cover him with canvas, forcing him to the ground. They carry him off, as he passes out.

13. What did Jessie think about as he stared at the black water the raft was travelling on?
    He thought of the fate of drowned people and wondered if his father's bones could lay somewhere nearby, white as chalk on the river bottom.

14. Where and when had Jessie seen one of his kidnappers before?
    He was a rough-looking sailor who had given Jessie two pennies to play a marital tune on his fife earlier that same day, down by the fruit stalls by the river.

The Moonlight

1. Where do Jessie's captors deposit him?
    He is deposited on a sailing ship named *The Moonlight*.

2. Which of Jessie's five senses was assaulted upon falling on the deck?
    His sense of smell. His nostrils were flooded with a smell so sickening, so menacing, it stopped his breath.

3. When Jessie expresses concern over his mother worrying, what does Purvis tell him?
    He tells him Claudius and he took care of it; that they spoke to her and told her they'd borrowed him for a while. Jessie knows it isn't true.

4. Describe Benjamin Stout.
    He is a tall, heavy-limbed man who treats Jessie fairly. He warns him to watch out for the first mate, Nicholas Spark, and to answer the Captain, even if he must lie.

5. Describe Captain Cawthorne.
    He is small man who is cruel, harsh, and unpredictable. Although an excellent seaman, he treats his crew and the Africans badly.

6. How does the Captain hurt Jessie and why?
    He bites his ear because he says he answers too quickly.

7. Where is the ship bound and for what purpose?
    It is bound for Africa to pick up slaves.

8. What does the Captain exchange the slaves for in Africa?
    The Captain exchanges money ($10 a head), rum, and tobacco for the slaves.

9. Why was Jessie needed?
   He is needed to play his instrument (fife) for the Africans to exercise; dance.

10. In what does Jessie sleep?
    He, and the other crew members must sleep in hammocks on the Tween deck.

11. Why do the British try to block the other slave traders?
    They had entirely stopped slave trading in their country and didn't want other countries continuing the practice.

12. What does Ben Stout say they're a dead ship without?
    He insists water is necessary.

13. Hunting and killing of what rodent was a daily ship routine?
    Rat hunts are a part of the ship's routine.

14. Describe Purvis.
    He is one of Jessie's kidnappers, a man who Jessie says resembles a very large frog. He takes a fondness for Jessie and teaches him many things on the ship.

The Shrouds

1. Other than the British, who else makes slave running hazardous?
   United States Revenue Cutters patrol the shores after privateers and smugglers who land slaves in Georgia and Florida.

2. What jobs filled up Jessie's days on the ship?
   He waited on the Captain, heaved waste over the side, mended sails, and tracked rats.

3. Jessie used to think the sea was always blue. What colors does he see now?
   A color that was like the smell of salt air, and at sundown, yellow as cane stalks, green as limes, and orange as shrimps.

4. When did Jessie become most fearful?
   During a rain squal Jessie was most fearful. He felt as if he was choking to death and sobbed with terror.

5. Even though Ben Stout treats Jessie well, who does Jessie prefer?
   He prefers and trusts Purvis over Stout.

6. What changes occurred on the ship once it had becalmed?
    Gratings had replaced the solid hatches over the holds, a huge cauldron appeared in Curry's galley, tempers flared among the men, and Cooley was making a whip.

7. While sleeping on the deck, what did Jessie see one night?
    A disguised figure crawling toward the aft, then returning holding an egg in one hand, creeping back the way it had come.

8. Who was wrongfully accused and punished by the Captain for stealing the egg?
    Purvis was flogged and tied to the shrouds.

9. When Jessie questioned Purvis about why he didn't turn in the real culprit, Stout, how did Purvis respond?
    He says that the officers wouldn't have cared about the truth and that the Captain had it in his mind that it was a time for a flogging to remind the men.

The Bight of Benin

1. How do slaving ships employ different flags to their advantage?
    The Captain kept more than one country's flag in his quarters. If the ship was stopped, he would run up another county's flag and bring out papers to prove ownership to the flag's country. Other counties' ships would do the same.

2. What does Purvis ask Jessie to do that he has not done since he'd been on the ship?
    Purvis asks Jessie to play a tune on his fife for he and Smith .

3. Upon sighting land, what disturbing view was seen?
    The land was on fire. The British had set fire to the barracoon, trying to deter the sale of slaves.

4. What does the fire remind Jessie of?
    It reminds him of a great fire in New Orleans that had burned up 107 houses three years ago. It had frightened him very much.

5. When does the crew get to go on land?
    They do not get off the ship. Only the Captain debarks.

6. Why is it necessary for Jessie to play his fife for the slaves?
    The slaves need music to dance to keep them healthy.

7. Upon seeing land, how does Jessie's mood change?
    He goes into a dark mood and sulks terribly. It bothers him to be so near land and not be able to get off.

8. Jessie's comment about the kidnapping of the slaves causes Purvis to react in what way?
    He compares these circumstances with those of his ancestors who came over from Ireland sixty years earlier locked in a hold and sold.

9. What is Jessie ordered to do with the rum he was told to fetch?
    He is ordered to pour it in one of the slave men's mouth.

10. How and when were the slaves loaded on the ship?
    Long canoes slid alongside *The Moonlight* at night and they were lifted up over the rails.

11. How long was *The Moonlight* at the Bight of Benin?
    It was there for one week.

12. For what reason is Jessie smacked by Ned?
    When a little black girl was carried to the rail and flung into the water by Spark, Jessie cried out. Ned then smacked him.

13. How many slaves has the crew loaded on *The Moonlight*?
    Close to one hundred slaves were aboard.

Nicholas Spark Walks On Water
1. For what reason did *The Moonlight* sail away from Wydah at night?
    So the slaves would not see the shore of their homeland disappearing.

2. Name the African tribe the blacks loaded on the ship are part of.
    They are Ashantis, probably captured in tribal wars with the Yoruba.

3. Which crew member admits to the evilness of slave trading?
    Ned admits it's all the Devil's work.

4. Name the three crew members seemingly untouched by the blacks' suffering.
    Captain Cawthorne, Spark, and Stout do not seem affected by the obvious suffering.

5. Explain Jessie's reaction to seeing the naked blacks herded onto the deck to be made to dance.
    He is mortified beyond anything he had ever imagined.

6. If the slaves will not dance, what happens to them?
    They are whipped till they rise, or their bare feet stepped on with Spark's booted heel.

7. How often must Jessie 'dance' the slaves?
    He must perform this service every other day for three groups of slaves.

8. Tell the fate of the screaming black woman.
    She was carried to the rail alive, and then flung up and over out to sea.

9. What realization does Jessie have that causes him to defy his orders to play his fife?
    He thinks he hates the slaves! Not to hear them! Not to smell them! Not to know of their existence!

10. How many of Stout's lashes did Jessie's defiance earn?
    He was lashed five times, per the Captain's orders.

11. What role did Stout play in the 'mad' black woman's fate according to Purvis?
    Stout is the only crew member who can speak the native language. He had that poor woman up on deck and she was weeping and wailing, then Stout would strike her across the face, and continue this until she fell on the deck in a fit. He was addling her mind with his tales. He created her madness, which he claimed was why he had her thrown overboard.

12. How is Jessie able to temporarily escape the horrors of the ship?
    He found some freedom in his mind by imagining he was in another place- home. He would recall every object in his room on Pirate's Alley.

13. When Jessie notices the black boy his age watching him, what does he do?
    He took his fife from his lips and whispered his name, Jessie, and pointed to himself. He then began to play his fife again so as not to attract Stout's attention.

14. Which crew member did the Captain punish for shooting a slave?
    First Mate, Nicholas Spark, was bound with a rope and pushed to the rail and there dropped over. Jessie swears just before he disappeared beneath the water, he took three steps.

15. Jessie questions Ned about his illness. What is his reply?
    He tells Jessie he has 'a touch of death' and then asks Jessie, "Haven't you heard of the wages of sin? Did you think they were gold?"

<u>The Spaniard</u>
1. Which crew member replaces the First Mate?
    Benjamin Stout takes on Spark's duties.

2. How does Jessie respond to Stout's questioning about the morale of the crew?
    He tells him he hates this ship, and refuses his extended hand.

3. How does Purvis characterize Stout to Jessie?
    Purvis says he is dead, that someone makes little dolls of him and sprinkles them with gunpowder and places one in every ship- and out at sea the doll grows till it looks like a sailor.

4. Where does Stout place Jessie's flute and what must Jessie do to retrieve it?
    He has obviously taken Jessie's flute during the night and tossed it into the holds. He lowers Jessie into the holds where the slaves are squeezed into and demands he find it.

5. In what manner does Purvis try to cheer up Jessie?
    He gets him to play cat's cradle with him.

6. What is the strange stirring Jessie sees in the water over the rail.
    He sees slowly turning on their backs, sharks, which he calls great white maggots with crescent mouths upon which are stitched horrible teeth. Cooley says," Snap us up like flies."

7. What is Sharkey's opinion about the slaves' shackles?
    He says the Captain is a fool for hanging on to them after they take them off the slaves because just having them on the ship can be evidence enough for punishment.

8. Describe the Spaniard and his slave.
    The Spaniard is a tall black-haired man wearing a very frilly and lacy shirt. His black slave kept his head bowed, as if it had grown that way.

9. Where does Jessie vow never to visit again if he ever makes it home?
    He says he will never again go to the slave market in New Orleans.

Ben Stout's Mistake
1. What chore was Jessie sent to the Captain's quarters to complete?
    He was sent to the Captain's quarters to fetch a chest.

2. How does the Captain reward Jessie for not knowing what is in the chest?
    The Captain hands him some biscuits.

3. What does the Captain point out to the Spaniard who comments,"A miracle!"
    The Captain points out the Spanish flag hoisted in the air.

4. What is in the chest and for what purpose?
    There are fancy clothes for the slaves to dress up in on their last night on board.

5. After the slaves are dressed, now what must they do?
    They are to drink rum and dance with the crew.

6. Why is the festivity halted?
    The Spaniard's slave spots a sail. The drunken Stout says it's an English ship and it won't cause any trouble. The Captain orders the American flag to be hoisted.

7. What revelation causes the Captain to order the slaves overboard?
    The overtaking ship and its convoy is American.

8. What act of nature takes over at this point?
    A storm breaks overhead causing the ship to shake

9. How did Jessie and the black boy avoid further danger?
    They hid in the hold.

10. After the boys awaken and Jessie climbs out to the deck, what does he see?
    The ship is awash up to the hatches; it is a disaster. Purvis is seen caught under the crashed mainmast, dead. Stout is caught in a tangled web of rope, dead. No one else is visible.

11. When Jessie goes back to the hold, he and the black boy wait out the storm. What do they do next?
    They flung the boom into the water, and took hold of it and together swam toward land.

12. What does Jessie think kept him going when he could only dog paw?
    He feels hope delivered him from the depths to the shore.

The Old Man

1. Name the first living thing the boys see upon reaching the shore in Mississippi.
    A crab runs across Jessie's ankle.

2. What words does Jessie say to himself while dog pawing from the ship to the shore?
    He thinks of his drowned father and the words he wanted to tell him "Oh, swim!"

3. Daniel tells Jessie what information about the bodies from the ship?
    He says "you won't find nobody, the sharks will crack their bones."

4. How did Jessie and Daniel spend their time with Daniel?
    They did chores, chased chickens, built a shelter, and played hide and seek.

5. Where does Ras go?
   Two black men come for him to take him to the North.

6. On their last day together, what piece of the ship did Ras and Jessie find on the beach?
   A piece of the ship's bow.

7. What does Jessie promise Daniel before he leaves?
   He promises not to tell anyone about him.

Home and After
1. What did Jessie fear the most on his journey home?
   Jessie dreaded the thought of coming across any snakes.

2. How many days did Jessie's trip home take?
   His trip lasted four days.

3. How does Jessie's mother handle his absence and return?
   She questions the market venders daily about him, begins to think him dead, and is terrified of the story he tells and the fate of the slaves.

4. What type of job does Jessie learn?
   He is apprenticed to an apothecary.

5. What happened to Jessie after moving to Rhode Island?
   He fought for the Union in the Civil War and spent time in Andersonville.

6. How was Jessie affected musically by his experience?
   He was unable to listen to any kind of music ever again. It reminded him of the horrible scene on the ship when he was forced to dance the slaves.

MULTIPLE CHOICE STUDY GUIDE/QUIZ QUESTIONS - *The Slave Dancer*

History ; The Errand

1. The Moonlight is a
    a. brand new song
    b. shipwrecked ship
    c. sunken sailboat
    d. sequel to Apollo 13

2. Jessie's mother is a
    a. seamstress
    b. waitress
    c. servant
    d. nurse

3. Betty is intolerant to the
    a. cold
    b. heat
    c. dampness
    d. pollen

4. Jessie imagines the fog is
    a. a ghost
    b. sweat from the Mississippi
    c. smoke on the water
    d. bringing his father back

5. This chapter takes place in
    a. Cuba
    b. Alabama
    c. Louisiana
    d. Africa

6. Earlier that day Jessie had been to the forbidden
    a. Congo Square
    b. French Quarter
    c. Lake Pontchartrain
    d. slave market

Study Guide/Quiz Questions- *The Slave Dancer* Multiple Choice Format Page 2

7. Jessie thinks Aunt Agatha
    a. loves him very much
    b. is concerned for him
    c. is disagreeable and mean
    d. can bake a great cake

8. Jessie's father
    a. drowned in the Mississippi
    b. deserted their family
    c. lived in Massachusetts
    d. fell off a tree stump

9. Jessie's mother needs
    a. someone to clean the house
    b. the fan fixed
    c. a new job
    d. candles to see her work at night

10. Aunt Agatha treats Jessie
    a. well
    b. kindly
    c. graciously
    d. none of the above

11. Near the rich families' walls, Jessie is reminded of
    a. his errand
    b. the slave, 'Star'
    c. his lateness
    d. how poor he is

12. While daydreaming of great wealth Jessie
    a. trips on his fife
    b. falls down a step
    c. is kidnapped
    d. walks into a wall

Study Guide/Quiz Questions- *The Slave Dancer* Multiple Choice Format Page 3

13. Staring into the black water from the raft, Jessie
    a. knows he will die
    b. plans his escape
    c. wants to become a pirate
    d. thinks of his father

14. One of Jessie's kidnappers
    a. paid him two pennies
    b. ate oranges at the dock
    c. had him play a martial tune
    d. all of the above

Study Guide/Quiz Questions- *The Slave Dancer* Multiple Choice Format Page 4

<u>The Moonlight</u>

1. Jessie's captors deposit him
    a. on a raft
    b. in the sea
    c. on a sailboat
    d. on a sailing ship

2. Which of Jessie's senses was assaulted when he hit the deck?
    a. smell
    b. hearing
    c. sight
    d. touch

3. When Jessie expresses concern over his mother worrying,
    a. Claudius laughs at him
    b. Purvis says he took care of it
    c. Stout pats him on the back
    d. Captain shouts at him

4. Benjamin Stout is
    a. sorry
    b. concerned
    c. fair
    d. all of the above

5. Choose the one description that does not fit the Captain.
    a. mean tempered
    b. unpredictable
    c. open minded
    d. excellent seaman

6. What does the Captain do to Jessie?
    a. He bites his ear for speaking too quickly.
    b. He hits him with a stool.
    c. He dumps a bucket over his head.
    d. He kicks him in the rear.

Study Guide/Quiz Questions- *The Slave Dancer* Multiple Choice Format Page 5

7. *The Moonlight* is bound for
    a. Cuba to get sugar cane
    b. South Carolina to pick up molasses
    c. Africa to pick up slaves
    d. New Orleans to deliver the slaves

8. The Captain will give what in exchange for the slaves?
    a. rum
    b. money
    c. tobacco
    d. all of the above

9. Jessie was needed to
    a. chase and catch the rats
    b. play his fife
    c. play with the young slave boys
    d. clean the decks

10. Jessie sleeps
    a. in a hammock
    b. on the floor
    c. in the bird's nest
    d. on the poop deck

11. The British try to blockade the other slave traders because
    a. they want the profits for themselves
    b. they want to add new ships to their fleet
    c. the queen ordered them to
    d. they have stopped doing it and want others to stop too

12. Ben Stout says they're a dead ship without
    a. the Captain
    b. food
    c. both b and d
    d. water

Study Guide/Quiz Questions- *The Slave Dancer* Multiple Choice Format Page 6

13. The crew has a routine of chasing and killing
    a. ratsf
    b. cockroaches
    c. beetles
    d. all of the above

14. Purvis is
    a. one of Jessie's kidnappers
    b. an educated man
    c. on his first sea voyage
    d. the Captain's pet

Study Guide/Quiz Questions- *The Slave Dancer* Multiple Choice Format Page 7

<u>The Shrouds</u>

1. Other than the British, who makes slave running hazardous?
    a. The Quakers
    b. The U. S. Revenue Cutters
    c. Blackbeard and his pirates
    d. all of the above

2. Choose the one job Jessie did not do on the ship during the day.
    a. track the rats
    b. mend sails
    c. cook meals
    d. heave waste over the side

3. Jessie used to think the sea was always blue, now he sees
    a. green
    b. yellow
    c. orange
    d. all of the above

4. Jessie felt as if he had stopped breathing and began to sob when
    a. the lightening storm hit
    b. Purvis was flogged
    c. Cooley was making the whip
    d. the Captain bit his ear

5. Ben Stout treats Jessie well, but he prefers and trusts
    a. Ned
    b. Claudius
    c. Purvis
    d. Curry

6. When the ship had becalmed, which of the following occurred?
    a. gratings replaced the solid hatches over the holds
    b. the men became testy with each other
    c. a huge cauldron appeared in Curry's galley
    d. all of the above

Study Guide/Quiz Questions- *The Slave Dancer* Multiple Choice Format Page 8

7. One night while Jessie slept on deck, he saw
    a. an eclipse of the moon
    b. someone steal an egg
    c. a ghostlike figure
    d. a fight between two of the crew

8. Who was wrongly accused and flogged for stealing the egg?
    a. Purvis
    b. Stout
    c. Jessie
    d. Ned

9. When Jessie questioned the one wrongly accused, how did he respond?
    a. I helped eat it, so there it is.
    b. It doesn't hurt anyway.
    c. The officers don't care for the truth, the Captain wanted to flog someone.
    d. The Captain don't like me.

Study Guide/Quiz Questions- *The Slave Dancer* Multiple Choice Format Page 9

<u>The Bight of Benin</u>

1. Slaving ships protect themselves from patrollers by
    a. outrunning them
    b. hoisting different flags
    c. providing false papers
    d. both b and c

2. Purvis asks Jessie
    a. to play a tune
    b. to empty the latrine buckets
    c. to feed the slaves
    d. go to sleep in his hammock

3. When the crew of *The Moonlight* sees land they also notice
    a. a Spanish clipper
    b. rain
    c. fire
    d. the slaves waiting

4. Jessie is reminded of
    a. the French Quarter
    b. his mother and Betty
    c. the 1837 fire in New Orleans
    d. the candles he was to fetch

5. The crew gets to get off the boat
    a. for two hours
    b. the next day
    c. in the mornings
    d. only at the final destination

6. Jessie must play his fife to
    a. exercise the crew
    b. dance the slaves
    c. satisfy the Captain
    d. practice for Mardi Gras

Study Guide/Quiz Questions- *The Slave Dancer* Multiple Choice Format Page 10

7. When Jessie sees the land, he
    a. goes into a dark mood
    b. jumps for joy
    c. runs off the plank
    d. compares it to New Orleans

8. Purvis heatedly brings up the mistreatment of his Irish ancestors when
    a. Claudius rattles a slave's shackles
    b. Ned takes up for the blacks
    c. the Captain calls him an Irish bucket
    d. Jessie criticizes the slave operation

9. Jessie is ordered to
    a. eat the beans
    b. pour rum down a slave's mouth
    c. fetch rum for the Captain
    d. empty the cauldron

10. The slaves arrive on *The Moonlight*
    a. at night
    b. shackled
    c. in long canoes
    d. all of the above

11. *The Moonlight* was in the Bight of Benin
    a. one month
    b. three days
    c. one week
    d. two weeks

12. Jessie was smacked by Ned for
    a. crying out
    b. not doing his job
    c. smiling at the slaves
    d. not playing his fife

13. The number of slaves on board was
    a. fifty
    b. seventy-five
    c. nearly one hundred
    d. forty

Study Guide/Quiz Questions *The Slave Dancer* Multiple Choice Format Page 11

<u>Nicholas Spark Walks On Water</u>

1. The Moonlight sailed away from Wydah at night so
    a. the Revenue Cutters couldn't find it
    b. the British blockade would be ahead of it
    c. the slaves wouldn't see their vanishing homeland
    d. none of the above

2. The African tribe the slaves are a part of is the
    a. Yorubas
    b. Ibos
    c. Ashantis
    d. Navajo

3. Name the crew member who admits slaving is the Devil's work.
    a. Purvis
    b. Stout
    c. Ned
    d. Jessie

4. Which crew members are not outwardly affected by the slaves' suffering?
    a. Stout
    b. Spark
    c. Cawthorne
    d. all of the above

5. Which word does not describe Jessie's feelings about the naked blacks herded to the deck?
    a. curious
    b. mortified
    c. embarrassed
    d. humiliated

6. If they will not dance, what happens to the slaves?
    a. They are whipped or stepped on.
    b. They get sent to the holds.
    c. They don't receive dinner
    d. They have to play the flute.

Study Guide/Quiz Questions- *The Slave Dancer* Multiple Choice Format Page 12

7. Jessie must "dance" the slaves
    a. once a day
    b. every other day
    c. twice a day
    d. once a week

8. The screaming black woman
    a. fainted near Jessie
    b. was tossed overboard
    c. slapped Stout
    d. hid in the corner

9. Jessie defies the Captain's orders to play when
    a. he realizes he hates the slaves
    b. Stout makes him furious
    c. Purvis tells him to
    d. he becomes scared

10. How many lashes did Jessie's defiance earn him?
    a. ten
    b. three
    c. four
    d. five

11. How was Stout able to take special advantage of the black woman?
    a. He treated her child well.
    b. He knew members of her family who came over earlier.
    c. He could speak her language.
    d. He could understand her pain.

12. Jessie is able to escape the horrors of the ship temporarily by
    a. reading
    b. recalling every detail of his Pirate Alley homeplace
    c. playing his flute alone
    d. learning how to mend sails

Study Guide/Quiz Questions- *The Slave Dancer* Multiple Choice Format Page 13

13. Jessie stopped playing his flute briefly, pointed to himself and whispered his name when
    a. Stout went to the Captain's room
    b. Purvis was coming on deck
    c. he noticed the black boy watching him
    d. the Captain was talking to Spark

14. Who does the Captain throw overboard for shooting one of the slaves?
    a. Stout
    b. Purvis
    c. Spark
    d. Claudius

15. Which crew member tells Jessie he has a 'touch of death'?
    a. Ned
    b. Purvis
    c. Stout
    d. Smith

Study Guide/Quiz Questions- *The Slave Dancer* Multiple Choice Format Page 14

<u>The Spaniard</u>

1. The Captain replaces the First Mate with
    a. Spark
    b. Stout
    c. Smith

2. When Stout offers Jessie his hand, Jessie
    a. thanks him
    b. shakes it vigorously
    c. turns and walks away

3. Purvis characterizes Stout as a
    a. dead man
    b. genius
    c. saint

4. Where has Stout put Jessie's flute?
    a. overboard
    b. in the holds
    c. in the Captain's quarters
    d. in the galley

5. What game does Purvis use to cheer up Jessie?
    a. tiddlywinks
    b. solitaire
    c. cat in the cradle

6. What does Jessie see as a stirring in the water overboard?
    a. sharks
    b. whales
    c. dolphins

7. Sharkey thinks the Captain
    a. is very greedy
    b. should keep all the shackles
    c. isn't giving the crew fair wages

Study Guide/Quiz Questions- *The Slave Dancer* Multiple Choice Format Page 15

8. The Spaniard wears what piece of apparel that draws Jessie's attention?
    a. sequined hat
    b. shiny gloves
    c. lacy, frilly shirt

9. If he ever makes it home, Jessie vows never to visit
    a. Aunt Agatha
    b. slave market
    c. Pirate's Alley
    d. Congo square

Study Guide/Quiz Questions- *The Slave Dancer* Multiple Choice Format Page 16

<u>Ben Stout's Mistake</u>

1. Jessie is sent to the Captain's quarters to get a
    a. chest
    b. whip
    c. mop
    d. candle

2. In a rare mood, the Captain offers Jessie
    a. eggs
    b. clothes
    c. rum
    d. biscuits

3. What does the Spaniard comment about the Spanish flag?
    a. "Genius!"
    b. "Bravo!"
    c. " A miracle!"
    d. "Good job!"

4. Packed away in the chest were
    a. crowns for the tribe leaders
    b. dressy clothes for the slaves to put on
    c. treats for the last night on board
    d. shackles for the next load

5. What are the slaves required to do?
    a. unload the molasses
    b. saw off their shackles
    c. dress up and dance
    d. sing for the Spaniard

6. The festivity ends because
    a. the Spaniard's slave spots an approaching ship
    b. a lightening bolt hits the deck
    c. the Captain becomes too drunk
    d. Jessie refuses to play

Study Guide/Quiz Questions- *The Slave Dancer* Multiple Choice Format Page 17

7. When it is apparent the ship is American
    a. the Spaniard jumps overboard
    b. the Captain orders the slaves overboard
    c. Stout swears it is a Spanish ship in disguise
    d. Spark gets out the paperwork

8. To make matters worse
    a. the crew hides below
    b. a shark is spotted nearby
    c. there is a mutiny
    d. a storm breaks overhead

9. Who hides in the hold with Jessie?
    a. the Spaniard's slave
    b. a black boy
    c. Ned
    d. Purvis

10. Which one of the following doesn't Jessie see when he emerges from the hold?
    a. The Captain
    b. Stout
    c. Purvis
    d. shore

11. Jessie and his companion
    a. jump in a lifeboat and row away
    b. run to find all the crew members
    c. fling the boom in the water and swim for shore
    d. climb up to the lookout to spot land

12. Jessie is a skilled swimmer making it easily to shore.
    a. true
    b. false

Study Guide/Quiz Questions-*The Slave Dancer* Multiple Choice Format Page 18

<u>The Old Man</u>

1. The first living thing the boys sight upon reaching Mississippi is
    a. an old black man
    b. a chicken
    c. a piglet
    d. a crab

2. The words Jessie said to himself while dog pawing were
    a. Don't stop!
    b. Mother!
    c. Oh, swim!
    d. Keep going!

3. Jessie wonders if the bodies will wash ashore when Daniel tells him
    a. not to think about it
    b. the sharks will crack their bones
    c. he already saw one of them
    d. it takes a week

4. How did Jessie and Daniel spend their time with Daniel?
    a. built a shelter out of branches
    b. chased chickens
    c. chores
    d. all of the above

5. Where does Ras go?
    a. He runs away.
    b. Daniel takes him away.
    c. Two black men came to take him north.
    d. He goes with Jessie.

6. On their last day together, what piece of the ship did Ras and Jessie find on the beach?
    a. water cask
    b. bow
    c. mainsail
    d. mast

Study Guide/Quiz Questions- *The Slave Dancer* Multiple Choice Format Page 19

7. What does Jessie promise Daniel before he leaves?
    a. He will always remember him.
    b. He won't try to find Ras.
    c. He will follow the route perfectly.
    d. He won't tell anybody about him.

Study Guide/Quiz Questions-*The Slave Dancer* Multiple Choice Format Page 20

<u>Home and After</u>

1. What Jessie feared the most on his journey was
   a. the dark
   b. snakes
   c. losing his way
   d. none of the above

2. How many days did Jessie's trip home take?
   a. four
   b. five
   c. three
   d. seven

3. Jessie's mother
   a. questioned the market venders daily for news of Jessie
   b. thought him dead
   c. couldn't bear the fate of the slaves
   d. all of the above

4. Jessie was apprenticed to
   a. an apothecary
   b. a printer
   c. a blacksmith
   d. a cooper

5. During the Civil War, Jessie spent time in
   a. Antietim
   b. Andersonville
   c. Atlanta
   d. Gettysburg

6. Jessie's experience caused him to cherish music even more.
   a. true
   b. false

ANSWER KEY: MULTIPLE CHOICE STUDY GUIDE QUESTIONS
The Slave Dancer

History; The Errand
1. B
2. A
3. C
4. B
5. C
6. D
7. C
8. A
9. D
10. D
11. B
12. C
13. D
14. D

The Moonlight
1. D
2. A
3. B
4. D
5. C
6. A
7. C
8. D
9. B
10. A
11. D
12. D
13. A
14. A

The Shrouds
1. B
2. C
3. D
4. A
5. C
6. D
7. B
8. A
9. C

The Bight of Benin
1. D
2. A
3. C
4. C
5. D
6. B
7. A
8. D
9. B
10. D
11. C
12. A
13. C

Nicholas Spark Walks On Water
1. C
2. C
3. C
4. D
5. A
6. A
7. B
8. B
9. A
10. D
11. C
12. B
13. C
14. C
15. A

The Spaniard
1. B
2. C
3. A
4. B
5. C
6. A
7. A
8. C
9. B

Ben Stout's Mistake
1. A   11. C
2. D   12. B
3. C
4. B
5. C
6. A
7. B
8. C
9. B
10. A

The Old Man
1. D
2. C
3. B
4. D
5. C
6. B
7. D

Home and After
1. B
2. A
3. D
4. A
5. B
6. B

PREREADING VOCABULARY WORKSHEETS

Vocabulary - *The Slave Dancer* **History; The Errand**

Part I: Using Prior Knowledge and Contextual Clues

Below are the sentences in which the vocabulary words appear in the text. Read the sentence. Use any clues you can find in the sentence combined with your prior knowledge, and write what you think the underlined words mean in the space provided.

1. Sometimes I touched a sewing needle with my finger and reflected how such a small object, so nearly weightless, could keep our little family from the poorhouse and provide us with enough food to sustain life-although there were times when we were barely *sustained*.

2. As for the fog, she observed how it softened the *clamor* from the streets and alleyways and kept the drunken riverboat men away from our section of the Vieux Carre.

3. The whole room was covered with a great swathe of apricot colored *brocade* supported by chairs to keep it from touching the floor.

4., 5. My mother replied that I was a *surly* boy who would grow up to be an *uncharitable* man.

6. He had been working on a snagboat, helping to clear away the tree stumps and other hidden debris that had made the river so *perilous* for the passage of steamboats.

7. "What an *undignified* way to earn your keep! Playing that silly pipe!

8. The air was faintly scented with the aroma of flowers which grew in such *profusion* inside the walled gardens that belonged to the rich families in our neighborhood.

9. Someday, I might become a rich *chandler* in a fine suit, with a thousand candles to hand if I needed them instead of three grudgingly given stubs.

10. I was tossed, then *trussed*, then lifted up and carried like a pig.

11. Sometimes there was a noisy flap of wings when we frightened a heron away from its night roost, sometimes a slither and damp muddy sigh as an otter, belly flat, headed into a pool of *fetid* water.

12. It was a sailor who only that afternoon had given me two pennies to play him a *martial* tune down near the fruit stalls by the river.

(Vocab. **History; The Errand** con't)

Part II: Determining the Meaning

Match the vocabulary words to their dictionary definitions. If there are words for which you cannot figure out the definition by contextual clues and by process of elimination, look them up in a dictionary.

___ 1. sustained   A. elaborate woven fabric with a raised design
___ 2. clamor   B. uproar
___ 3. brocade   C. hard hearted
___ 4. surly   D. tasteless
___ 5. uncharitable   E. supported
___ 6. perilous   F. testy
___ 7. undignified   G. excess
___ 8. profusion   H. dangerous
___ 9. chandler   I. candle and supplies trader
___10. trussed   J. tied up
___11. fetid   K. military; warlike
___12. martial   L. foul

Vocabulary - *The Slave Dancer* **The Moonlight**

Part I: Using Prior Knowledge and Contextual Clues

Below are the sentences in which the vocabulary words appear in the text. Read the sentence. Use any clues you can find in the sentence combined with your prior knowledge, and write what you think the underlined words mean in the space provided.

1. I was in danger of *decapitation* from the wooden arm to which the sail was attached, and which swung unexpectedly from side to side.

2. "Purvis is an Irish bucket," the thin man said *reflectively* as though he'd only just thought of it himself.

3. We were sailing to Africa, the Captain repeated with a *lofty* gesture of his hand.

4. And this fast little clipper would keep us safe not only from the British, but from any misguided pirates who would try to interfere in the *lucrative* and God-granted trade of slaves.

5. He, Captain Cawthorne, would purchase as many slaves as possible from the *barracoon* in Whydah, exchanging for them both money, $10 a head, and rum and tobacco.

6. "I let you sleep because you had such a *harrowing* night of it, but you'll be put to work soon enough."

7. *Mortified*, I opened my eyes at once to see who was observing me, for I assumed the laughter was at my expense.

8. "I saw Saint Stout pass you that bread, and if I fancied I could have him *flogged* for that."

9. "I should like to find out who makes these things," he said *pensively*, as his fist fell.

10. "You'll have to be *spry* to run after the rats down there, " he said.

11. "Ah, it's the British who've forced me to be so *ingenious*."

(Vocab. **The Moonlight** con't)

Part II: Determining the Meaning

　　　　Match the vocabulary words to their dictionary definitions. If there are words for which you cannot figure out the definition by contextual clues and by process of elimination, look them up in a dictionary.

Match the vocabulary words to their dictionary definitions.

___ 13. decapitation　　　A. noble
___ 14. reflectively　　　B. brilliant
___ 15. lofty　　　　　　C. shamed; embarrassed
___ 16. lucrative　　　　D. deliberately
___ 17. barracoon　　　　E. profitable
___ 18. harrowing　　　　F. thoughtfully
___ 19. mortified　　　　G. frightening
___ 20. flogged　　　　　H. beheading
___ 21. pensively　　　　I. lashed; whipped
___ 22. spry　　　　　　 J. limber; agile
___ 23. ingenious　　　　K. enclosure of slaves

Vocabulary - *The Slave Dancer* **The Shrouds**

Part I: Using Prior Knowledge and Contextual Clues
Below are the sentences in which the vocabulary words appear in the text. Read the sentence. Use any clues you can find in the sentence combined with your prior knowledge, and write what you think the underlined words mean in the space provided.

1. At first, these hard facts had been clouded over by the crew's *protestations* that the sheer number of ships devoted to the buying and selling of Africans was so great that it cancelled out American laws against the trade.

2. But when I discovered that Ned, like all the rest of the men, held a share of the profit to be realized from the sale of the blacks. I paid little attention to his pretense of *aloofness*.

3. I knew it must be Purvis on the watch, for while I was idly counting stars, a great wad of *vile* brown stuff flew by my ear as he expelled his gob of chewing tobacco over the side.

4. We had been at sea now for nearly three weeks when one morning after the deck had been *holystoned* the wind dropped entirely

5. The sun seemed *impaled* by the mizzenmast.

6. There was no getting used to it for me- living the ordinary life of an eating and sleeping creature but on a thing that always moved, a wooden thing whose fate could be changed by a shift of the wind, a sudden piling up of *briny* water, by currents and rain.

7.,8. But this time, it crawled along on only three limbs for one hand was held up, its *begrimed* fingers holding a beautiful white egg which, in that dim light, was as *luminous* as a tiny moon rising between deck and rail.

9. "But then you see," he continued *amiably* as though discussing the best way to splice a rope, "Purvis and me has sailed with the Captain and Spark before and I believe they favor me a bit over him."

10. Why didn't they go to the captain and inform him of the real *culprit*?

(Vocab. **The Shrouds** con't)

Part II: Determining the Meaning

Match the vocabulary words to their dictionary definitions. If there are words for which you cannot figure out the definition by contextual clues and by process of elimination, look them up in a dictionary.

___ 24. protestations
___ 25. aloofness
___ 26. vile
___ 27. holystoned
___ 28. impaled
___ 29. briny
___ 30. begrimed
___ 31. luminous
___ 32. amiably
___ 33. culprit

A. scrubbed clean by a soft sandstone
B. guilty party
C. glowing; radiant
D. salty sea water
E. fenced in
F. indifference
G. foul
H. grimy; filthy
I. pleasantly
J. objections

Vocabulary - *The Slave Dancer* **The Bight of Benin**

Part I: Using Prior Knowledge and Contextual Clues

Below are the sentences in which the vocabulary words appear in the text. Read the sentence. Use any clues you can find in the sentence combined with your prior knowledge, and write what you think the underlined words mean in the space provided.

1. The result of his labor was a platform on which squatted a nine-pound *carronade*, black as a bat, absorbing sunlight or the white glare of sunless days, an iron presence which Nicholas Spark touched each time he passed it as though for luck.

2. The *armament* was enough.

3. My friend was a man who *pressganged* me.

4. "Play us a tune," Purvis' voice floated up to me with a certain *melancholy* note.

5. "We won't never land," he said angrily as though I'd been *impertinent*.

6. "And it makes any Captain wild to *jettison* the sick ones within sight of the marketplace itself after all the trouble he's gone to."

7. Not for the last time, I considered casting myself over the side and *confounding* them all!

8. Ben, reading his small Bible by oil lamp with an *aggrieved* but forgiving look on his face.

9. Purvis and I watched them go into the Captain's quarters. "That's the *cabociero*," said Purvis.

10. And I looked with growing fear toward that shore which lay behind the *turbulent* waves whose ghostly white crests were visible in the darkness.

11. Although many were silent now, some continued to *lament*.

12. I had a new job-to empty the bucket latrines as they were handed up to me by Benjamin Stout who, moving across the *recumbent* bodies in the holds, went about his work as though stepping on cobblestones.

(Vocab. **The Bight of Benin** con't)

Part II: Determining the Meaning

Match the vocabulary words to their dictionary definitions. If there are words for which you cannot figure out the definition by contextual clues and by process of elimination, look them up in a dictionary.

___ 34. carronade   A. mournful
___ 35. armament   B. forced into ship service
___ 36. pressganged C. abandon; get rid of
___ 37. melancholy   D. leaning; idle
___ 38. impertinent E. arms; weapons
___ 39. jettison   F. puzzling; flustering
___ 40. confounding G. small cannon
___ 41. aggrieved   H. pained
___ 42. cabociero   I. roaring; blustery
___ 43. turbulent   J. Portuguese slave broker
___ 44. lament   K. sassy; fresh
___ 45. recumbent   L. wail; sob

Vocabulary - *The Slave Dancer* **Nicholas Spark Walks on Water**

Part I: Using Prior Knowledge and Contextual Clues

Below are the sentences in which the vocabulary words appear in the text. Read the sentence. Use any clues you can find in the sentence combined with your prior knowledge, and write what you think the underlined words mean in the space provided.

1. I knew now how the crew responded to any sign of my distress at the *plight* of the slaves.

2. Not all the gabble of the sailors, the sustained flow of the wind that drove us on, could mask the *keening* of the slaves as they twisted and turned on the water casks.

3., 4. "The African was tempted and then became *depraved* by a desire for the material things offered him by *debased* traders. It's all the Devil's work."

5. Why I was *chagrined* in one instance and hilarious in another, I don't know.

6. But what I felt now, now that I could gaze without *restraint* at the helpless and revealed forms of these slaves, was a mortification beyond any I had ever imagined.

7. Most of them had what Purvis called the bloody flux, an agonizing *affliction* of their bowels.

8. I thought of the slaves, of the violent hatred I had felt for them that had so frightened me that I had *defied* Master and his crew.

9. I shuddered at the *barbarousness* of chance which had brought each of them to our holds.

10. You can be sure he *addles* their minds with his tales.

11. I could not *relinquish* my dream of home.

12. "Old Cawthorne's been through *mutinies* before. He never lost a hair!" replied Purvis.

(Vocab. **Nicholas Spark Walks on Water** con't)

Part II: Determining the Meaning

Match the vocabulary words to their dictionary definitions. If there are words for which you cannot figure out the definition by contextual clues and by process of elimination, look them up in a dictionary.

___ 46. plight
___ 47. keening
___ 48. depraved
___ 49. debased
___ 50. chagrined
___ 51. restraint
___ 52. affliction
___ 53. defied
___ 54. barbarousness
___ 55. addles
___ 56. relinquish
___ 57. mutinies

A. Revolts; uprisings
B. Boldly resisted
C. Disease
D. Give up
E. Sorry situation
F. Confuses
G. Horribly cruel
H. Control; restriction
I. Annoyed
J. Wailing; mourning
K. Dishonorable
L. Corrupted

Vocabulary *The Slave Dancer* **The Spaniard**

Part I: Using Prior Knowledge and Contextual Clues

Below are the sentences in which the vocabulary words appear in the text. Read the sentence. Use any clues you can find in the sentence combined with your prior knowledge, and write what you think the underlined words mean.

1. And although Ben Stout could and did increase our misery with his *captious* orders, there was a limit

2. Though we were out of the *doldrums*, Purvis never left off exclaiming at our luck in not having been becalmed for weeks.

3. Despite my intention, I could not but see the wretched *shambling* men and women whose shoulders sank and rose in exhausted imitation of movement.

4. "I'd like a word with you," he said, *wheedling* now.

5. Only pirates might take us, French pirates *undeterred* by any flag.

6. I could barely draw breath, and what breath I drew was horrible, like a solid substance, like suet, that did not free my lungs but drowned them in the taste of *rancid* rot.

7. The two of them went to the Captain's quarters in front of which the black man stood like a *sentinel.*

Part II: Determining the Meaning

Match the vocabulary words to their dictionary definitions. If there are words for which you cannot figure out the definition by contextual clues and by process of elimination, look them up in a dictionary.

___ 58. captious
___ 59. doldrums
___ 60. shambling
___ 61. wheedling
___ 62. undeterred
___ 63. rancid
___ 64. sentinel

A. Rotten; foul
B. Unstopped
C. Shuffling
D. Charming or coaxing; flattering
E. Guard
F. Region of calm winds near the equator
G. Faultfinding

Vocabulary *The Slave Dancer* **Ben Stout's Mistake**

Part I: Using Prior Knowledge and Contextual Clues
    Below are the sentences in which the vocabulary words appear in the text. Read the sentence. Use any clues you can find in the sentence combined with your prior knowledge, and write what you think the underlined words mean.

1. There was a smoky *indistinct* look to the Cuban shore.

2. A loud grunt left me *perplexed* as to what to do.

3. "Ready for what?" I asked. "For the *festivity*," said Stout grinning.

4. It was a sight that was both heartrending and *ludicrous*, for the black people were not resisting.

5. Stout was picking up armfuls of clothes and flinging them at the blacks who stood silently and *impassively.*

6. Now the slaves, aware of their *mortal* danger, sank down, piling themselves up on one another as though in this way they could protect themselves.

7. I began to wail like a *demented* person.

8. As I sat, braced against the howling, crashing *chaos* above, I took some comfort in the small but steady sound of the black boy's breathing.

9. The mainmast lay *athwart* the deck, broken and twisted, its sails all rags.

10. I thought I heard a cry for help but the wind *mimicked* distress so perfectly there was no way to tell.

11. I felt a monstrous *convulsion* traveling through what was left of *The Moonlight*.

12. Waves washed *placidly* across the ship.

(Vocab. **Ben Stout's Mistake** con't))

Part II: Determining the Meaning

    Match the vocabulary words to their dictionary definitions. If there are words for which you cannot figure out the definition by contextual clues and by process of elimination, look them up in a dictionary.

___ 65. indistinct	A. Puzzled
___ 66. perplexed	B. Celebration
___ 67. festivity	C. Unclear
___ 68. ludicrous	D. Confusion; disorder
___ 69. impassively	E. Deadly; fatal
___ 70. mortal	F. Crosswise; at right angles to the ship's keel
___ 71. demented	G. Ridiculous
___ 72. chaos	H. Crazy; mad
___ 73. athwart	I. Without expression
___ 74. mimicked	J. Peacefully
___ 75. convulsion	K. Contraction; shaking
___ 76. placidly	L. Imitated

Vocabulary - *The Slave Dancer* **The Old Man; Home and After**

Part I: Using Prior Knowledge and Contextual Clues

Below are the sentences in which the vocabulary words appear in the text. Read the sentence. Use any clues you can find in the sentence combined with your prior knowledge, and write what you think the underlined words mean in the space provided.

1. The *tranquil* sea was turning from gray to a mild blue as the sun's pale rays spread out over the water.

2. He started to pull off the garment when something caught his attention in the long *defile* of palms above the beach.

3. Behind the palms was the thick dark green of what appeared to be *impenetrable* underbrush.

4. On land at last, in a silence broken only by insects chirring, warmed by the damp breathless heat of the forest around us, resting on a surface that remained steady, about to *assuage* my hunger, I couldn't understand the heaviness that weighed me down, that made it so difficult to breathe.

5. We found, resting amid the sea *wrack* at the high water line, a curved piece of the ship's bow.

6. The dawn's light was still too weak to *penetrate* the forest, although when I looked straight up, I could see the paling of the sky.

7. The smell of the ashes had been *revivified* by the morning dew.

8. I followed it until I came to the place where two tall columns marked the beginning of another road which ran straight as a *plumb* line to the steps of a great plantation house.

9. Suddenly, moved by an *obscure* impulse, I held my breath.

10. I was finally apprenticed to an *apothecary.*

11. It would be a different future from the one I had once *envisaged* when I had wanted to become a rich chandler.

12. I dreamed of the long muddy Mississippi and *languorous* green twilights and the old amber and apricot colored walls of the houses of the rich in the Vieux Carre.

(Vocab. **The Old Man; Home and After** con't)

Part II: Determining the Meaning

Match the vocabulary words to their dictionary definitions. If there are words for which you cannot figure out the definition by contextual clues and by process of elimination, look them up in a dictionary.

___ 77. tranquil
___ 78. defile
___ 79. impenetrable
___ 80. assuage
___ 81. wrack
___ 82. penetrate
___ 83. revivified
___ 84. plumb
___ 85. obscure
___ 86. apothecary
___ 87. envisaged
___ 88. languorous

A. sleepy; lazy
B. gully; ravine
C. ease; relieve
D. dense; thick
E. seaweed
F. unknown; unfamiliar
G. enter; come through
H. peaceful
I. pictured
J. rekindled; revived
K. absolute; exact
L. druggist; pharmacist

ANSWER KEY: VOCABULARY
The Slave Dancer

History; The Errand
1. E
2. B
3. A
4. F
5. C
6. H
7. D
8. G
9. I
10. J
11. L
12. K

The Moonlight
13. H
14. D
15. A
16. E
17. K
18. G
19. C
20. I
21. F
22. J
23. B

The Shrouds
24. J
25. F
26. G
27. A
28. E
29. D
30. H
31. C
32. I
33. B

The Bight of Benin
34. G
35. E
36. B
37. A
38. K
39. C
40. F
41. H
42. J
43. I
44. L
45. D

Nicholas Spark Walks On Water
46. E
47. J
48. L
49. K
50. I
51. H
52. C
53. B
54. G
55. F
56. D
57. A

The Spaniard
58. G
59. F
60. C
61. D
62. B
63. A
64. E

Ben Stout's Mistake
65. C
66. A
67. B
68. G
69. I
70. E
71. H
72. D
73. F
74. L
75. K
76. J

The Old Man; Home and After
77. H
78. B
79. D
80. C
81. E
82. G
83. J
84. K
85. F
86. L
87. I
88. A

DAILY LESSONS

LESSON ONE

Objectives
1. To give students background information for *The Slave Dancer*
2. To give students the opportunity to fulfill their nonfiction reading assignment that goes along with this unit
3. To give students practice using library resources
4. To prepare students for the introductory activity in Lesson Two.
5. To give students the opportunity to write to inform by developing and organizing facts to convey information.

Activity

Assign one of each of the following topics to each of your students. Some topics will require a pair of students, or a small group to research. Distribute Writing Assignment #1. Discuss the directions in detail. Take your students to the library so they may work on the assignment. Students should fill out a "Nonfiction Assignment Sheet" for at least one of the sources they used, and students should submit these sheets with their compositions.

Topics
1. Locate the state of Louisiana. Find the city of New Orleans and its French Quarter, Lake Pontchartrain, Lake Borge, Baratarian Bay, and the Mississippi River.
2. Were New Orleans and Louisiana always a part of the U.S.A?
4. Define Creole.
5. What is a Quaker? What are their beliefs?
6. Where are Whydah, the Bight of Benin, and the Gulf of Guinea located? What other name is this area given?
7. Locate Cuba and the West Indies. Describe their climate.
8. Locate the island of Sao Tome. What is distinct about its location?
9. What is a slave market? What is Congo Square in New Orleans?
10. Where is Charleston? Why would molasses be an important delivery there in the 1840's?
11. When was the Civil War? What were the issues? Where was Andersonville and what is it known for?
12. Describe the similarities and differences among these fabrics: brocade, silk, muslin, lace, damask, gauze, and velvet.
13. Make a timeline of slave trading starting with the 1500's through 1860's.
14. Who are the Ashantis? Yorubas? Ibos? Compare their cultures.
16. What was the British Blockade? U. S. Revenue Cutters?
17. What is a levee, a bayou?
18. What are doldrums? Where do they geographically occur?
19. Where is Cape Verde located? Describe its geography.
20. Name three of the Great Empires of West Africa.
21. Where and what is the Middle Passage?

22. How did the Underground Railroad operate? Name its most well-known conductor.
23. What was an abolitionist?
24. Define the following nautical terms and identify their location or use on a ship: aft, berth, boatswain, boom, bow, bowsprit, brail, bulwark, cargo, cathead, clipper, compass, davits, deck, fid, gaff, galley, hatch, helm, helmsman, holds, hull, keel, knot, mast, masthead, mizzenmast, poop deck, port, ratlines, rigging, sailyard, shrouds, skiff, starboard, stern, tarpaulin, topmast, yards, and yaw.

WRITING ASSIGNMENT #1 - *The Slave Dancer*

PROMPT

You are going to read a story about a boy your age from New Orleans who goes on an errand for his mother, and does not return for many months. It takes place in the 1840's in the South, a time of slave trading. It is realistic or historical fiction (the events in the novel *could* have taken place, but the characters and events are *fictional*). Before you read it, however, you should have some background information about some of the places and things mentioned in the story.

You have been assigned one topic about which you must find information. You are to read as much as you can about that topic and write a composition in which you relate what you have learned from your reading. Note that this is a *composition*, not just a sentence or two.

PREWRITING

You will go to the library. When you get there, use the library's resources to find information about your topic. Look for books, encyclopedias, articles in magazines- anything that will give you the information you require. Take a few notes as you read to help you remember important dates, names, places, or other details that will be important in your composition.

After you have gathered information and become well-read on the subject of your report, make a little outline, putting your facts in order.

DRAFTING

You will need an introductory paragraph in which you introduce your topic.

In the body of your composition, put the "meat" of your research- the facts you found- in paragraph form. Each paragraph should have a topic sentence (a sentence letting the reader know what the paragraph will be about) followed by an explanation, examples or details.

Write a concluding paragraph in which you summarize the information you found and conclude your report.

PROMPT

After you have finished a rough draft of your paper, revise it yourself until you are happy with your work. Then, ask a student who sits near you to tell you what he/she likes best about your work, and what things he/she thinks can be improved. Take another look at your composition, keeping in mind your critic's suggestions, and make the revisions you feel are necessary.

PROOFREADING

Do a final proofreading of your paper double-checking your grammar, spelling, organization, and the clarity of your ideas.

NONFICTION ASSIGNMENT SHEET - *The Slave Dancer*
(To be completed after reading the required nonfiction article)

Name _____ Date _____

Title of Nonfiction Read _____

Written By _____ Publication Date _____

I. Factual Summary: Write a short summary of the piece you read.

II. Vocabulary
    1. With which vocabulary words in the piece did you encounter some degree of difficulty?

    2. How did you resolve your lack of understanding with these words?

III. Interpretation: What was the main point the author wanted you to get from reading his work?

IV. Criticism
    1. With which points of the piece did you agree or find easy to accept? Why?

    2. With which points of the piece did you disagree or find difficult to believe? Why?

V. Personal Response: What do you think about this piece? OR How does this piece influence your ideas?

LESSON TWO

Objectives
1. To introduce *The Slave Dancer* unit
2. To check students' nonfiction reading assignments

Note: Prior to this class please post a world map, a map of Louisiana, including New Orleans, and a ship sketch, posted on your bulletin board. If you do not have a bulletinboard to use, use your chalkboard, an easel, a wall or a combination.

Activity #1
     Provide students with a plain file card, posterboard strip, or something similar. Have each of them write one fact he/she learned from his/her research. Students could briefly illustrate their fact card, if time allows. Have students one by one, bring their fact up to or near a map and post it. Encourage accurate placement for an attractive display. Students could also write directly on the bulletinboard paper. Those who researched the ship terms, need to label directly on the sketch, some terms may need to be illustrated. After they have placed their fact up, have them share. Discuss each fact briefly as it is presented so all students will be exposed to a wide variety of background information before reading. After all have shared, ask students to brainstorm a **name** for their display based on the information generated. Post title.

TRANSITION: After all students have had the opportunity to share, ask them how they would like spending endless months on a slaving ship in the 1840's against their will. Tell them tomorrow they will find out how one such young man got involved in this gruesome adventure.

LESSON THREE

Objectives
1. To distribute books and other related materials
2. To model effective oral reading skills by reading aloud pages 1-mid 8
3. To have students identify setting and point of view

Activity #1
Distribute the materials students will use in this unit and explain how they are to be used.

Study Guides Students should preview the study guide questions before each reading assignment to get a feeling for what events and ideas are important in that section. After reading the section, students will (as a class or individually) answer the questions to review the important events and ideas from that section of the book. Students should keep the study guides as study materials for the unit test.

Vocabulary Prior to reading a reading assignment, students will do vocabulary work related to the section of the book they are about to read. Following the completion of the reading of the book, there will be a vocabulary review of all the words used in the vocabulary assignments. Students should keep their vocabulary work as study materials for the unit test.

Reading Assignment Sheet You need to fill in the reading assignment sheet to let students know when their reading has to be completed. You can either write the assignment sheet on a side blackboard or bulletin board and leave it there for students to see each day, or you can make copies for each student to have.

Extra Activities Center The unit resource section of this unit contains suggestions for a library of related books and articles in your classroom as well as crossword and word search puzzles. Make an extra activities center in your room where you will keep these materials for students to use. (Bring the books and articles in from the library and keep several copies of the puzzles on hand.) Explain to students that these materials are available for students to use when they finish reading assignments or other class work early

Books Each school has its own rules and regulations regarding student use of school books. Advise students of the procedures that are normal for your school.

Activity #2
Have students examine the cover of the book and turn to page viii; History. Read this and the next seven and one-half pages to them as they follow along. (Stop with 'covering me entirely, forcing me to the ground' on page 8.) Identify the use of first person narration. Emphasize earlier covered locations presented now within the context. Encourage students to close their eyes and try to visualize the scenes while you read. Assign P, V, R for the remainder of "The Errand."

LESSON FOUR

Objectives
1. To review the main events and vocabulary from "History" and "The Errand"
2. To preview the study questions for "The Moonlight"
3. To familiarize students with the vocabulary in "The Moonlight"
4. To begin the reading of "The Moonlight"

Activity #1

Review the vocabulary from "The Errand" by reproducing the matching section on the chalkboard or on an overhead transparency. Have students volunteer to come up and find the correct match for each vocabulary word. After they have made the match, ask them to use the word in an original sentence. Also have them identify its part of speech.

Activity #2

Discuss the answers to the study questions for "History" and "The Errand" in detail. Write the answers on the board or overhead transparency so students can have the correct answers for study purposes. Note: It is a good practice in public speaking and leadership skills for individual students to take charge of leading the discussions of the study questions. Perhaps a different student could go to the front of the class and lead the discussion each day that the study questions are discussed during this unit. Of course, the teacher should guide the discussion when appropriate and be sure to fill in any gaps the students leave.

Activity #3

Give students the remaining class time to preview the study questions for "The Moonlight" and to do the related vocabulary work. If time allows, begin reading "The Moonlight" or assign the reading of it to be completed prior to the next class session.

LESSON FIVE

<u>Objectives</u>
1. To review the main events and ideas from "The Moonlight"
2. To practice identifying characters through the use of their speech
3. To review and practice vocabulary from "The Moonlight"
4. To review ship terminology from Lesson Two
5. To preview study questions and vocabulary from "The Shrouds"

<u>Activity #1</u>
Discuss the answers to the study questions for "The Moonlight" as you have done the study questions previously.

<u>Activity #2</u>
Allow each student to select a partner. Have them take turns reading quotes to each other to identify the speaker out of "The Errand" and "The Moonlight". Encourage them to try to sound like the person whose quote it is by acting some out yourself and having them guess.

<u>Activity #3</u>
Have students look over the prereading vocabulary work for The Shrouds for about 10 minutes. Use the matching section of the vocabulary pages from "The Moonlight" and" The Shrouds" as a springboard for a game similar to Concentration. Divide students into groups of four or five. Have students quickly copy the vocabulary words (divide the task into sections to expedite) and their clues on separate index cards. (This could be done prior to lesson to save time.) Turn them all over, after mixing them up. Have students in small groups take turns flipping over two of the cards. If they are a match, i.e. a vocabulary word matches with its meaning, they keep the pair and get another turn. Students may look at the vocabulary words in their sentences for contextual clues. Continue play until all cards are matched into sets. Play again, if time. Play could be separated by chapters, or combined according to the level of your students.

<u>Activity #4</u>
In preparation for the upcoming reading, review the ship terminology from Lesson Two. One way would be to play " pin the word on the ship". Have cards or slips of paper with the earlier listed terms and lead students into positioning them accurately . You could have tape on the back or use thumb tacks to have them stick. (Blindfolding would be a bit tricky!)

<u>Activity #5</u>
If time, have students look over study questions for "The Shrouds". Assign P, R of "The Shrouds" to be done prior to the next class session.

LESSON SIX

Objectives
1. To review the main events and ideas of "The Shrouds"
2. To review the map locations presented in Lesson Two
3. To begin characterization of main novel characters

Activity #1

Use the multiple choice format of the study guide questions for "The Shrouds" as a quiz to check that students have done the required reading and to review the main ideas of this chapter. Exchange papers for checking. Discuss answers and make sure students take notes for studying purposes.

Activity #2

Using maps review locations discussed in Lesson Two.

Activity #3

Duplicate either characterization chart from the next two pages on the chalkboard or the overhead. Place Jessie's name in the boat or at top of the table. Fill out as a class; guiding their responses based on specific examples of character's **physical traits**, **actions**, **speech**, and **thoughts** or **feelings** (if known, Jessie's are). Hand out blank chart to class. If using the ship, just write within the sail where the topic is written. On the table, list in blocks beneath topic. Students need to copy the information from this one when you have completed it.

Activity #4

Divide the class into nine small groups or pairs, depending on the # of students. Hand out only one chart per group. Have each group assign a recorder. Give each group one of the following characters to chart based on the first three chapters: Captain Cawthorne, Nicholas Spark, Ben Stout, Clay Purvis, John Cooley, Adolf Curry, Ned Grime, Claudius Sharkey, and Seth Smith. Inform them that there is not an equal amount of information on each character, so all charts will not contain the same amount of information.

Activity #5

Have students select a representative from each of their groups to share their group's character chart with the class. Have all students summarize information for all characters. Each student will need ten copies (use back and front). Be sure students save charts for future use and reference. If time runs out, students may continue during time you are doing conferences in the next lesson.

NOTE: Explain to students that you will be having writing conferences in the next class session. During the writing conference, you will discuss their writing skills individually, based on their first writing assignment in this unit.

CHARACTER CHART

for _____ _____
                   name   job on ship

Physical traits	Actions	Feelings; thoughts	Speech

LESSON SEVEN

Objectives
1. To preview the vocabulary and study guide questions for "The Bight of Benin"
2. To silently read "The Bight of Benin"
3. To evaluate students' writing
4. To have students revise their Writing Assignment 1 papers

Activity #1
Assign the prereading vocabulary pages, study guide questions and reading of "The Bight of Benin". Students should work on this independently while they are waiting for their conference with you.

Activity #2
Call students to your desk (or some other private area) to discuss their papers from Writing Assignment 1. Use the following Writing Evaluation Form to help structure your conference. Give students a date when their revisions are due.

WRITING EVALUATION FORM - *The Slave Dancer*

Name _____ Date _____

Writing Assignment #1 for *The Slave Dancer* unit   Grade _____

Circle One For Each Item:

Description (paragraph 1)	excellent	good	fair	poor
Plans (body paragraphs)	excellent	workable	fair	not realistic
Conclusion	excellent	good	fair	poor
Grammar:	excellent	good	fair	poor (errors noted)
Spelling:	excellent	good	fair	poor (errors noted)
Punctuation:	excellent	good	fair	poor (errors noted)
Legibility:	excellent	good	fair	poor

Strengths:

Weaknesses:

Comments/Suggestions:

LESSON EIGHT

Objectives
1. To review and practice vocabulary and main events and ideas from "The Bight of Benin"
2. To do the prereading vocabulary work for "Nicholas Spark Walks On Water"
3. To preview study guide questions for "Nicholas Spark Walks On Water"

Activity #1

Hand out four little slips of paper or mini cards to each student that have the letters A,B,C, or D on them. A good idea is to use different color cards for each letter. Use the multiple choice study guide questions and answers on "The Bight of Benin" for an oral review. Read the question (and/ or show it on the overhead). Then give students the four possible answers, labeling them A, B, C, or D (or show on overhead again). Students respond by holding up the card with what they think is the correct answer. This is one variety of Every Student Response. Remind students not to look at what others are holding up, but to simply display the card of their choice. This is a quick indicator of students' comprehension. You can make it somewhat different by requiring complete silence and having them read the questions silently from the overhead, or make it more mysterious (fun?) by blindfolding everyone and have them hold up a certain number of fingers per answer instead of using the cards.

Activity #2

Have students pair up. Using easels (if available) or scrap/drawing paper, one student draws an impression of one of the vocabulary words, while the other person tries to guess which word it is. After identifying correctly, students need to use words in an original sentence. Continue play until all vocabulary from "The Bight of Benin" has been covered. Students may use their prereading vocabulary sheets as a resource for this activity.

Activity #3

Have students begin the prereading vocabulary work and the preview of study guide questions for "Nicholas Spark Walks On Water" independently in remaining time. Inform them these items need completed by next class session.

LESSON NINE

Objectives
    1. To introduce simile, personification, and metaphor as figures of speech
    2. To distinguish between three different types of figurative language/ literary devices
    3. To have students locate figurative language in the text
    4. To create original figures of speech
    5. To illustrate figurative language

Activity #1

    Tell the class you are going to read a few phrases to them from their most recently read chapter in the book. Ask them to listen carefully and try to identify similarities between them or see if they can identify what they are examples of:
- On a platform squatted a nine-pound carronade, black as a bat.
- The two men danced, circling each other like two dreaming bears, their faces as serious as though they were reading the Bible.
- Sheets of flame as red and jagged as the wounds the rope had opened in Purvis' back flew upward into a darkening sky.
- "I can't hang here like a ham for smoking."
- Three days we sat there like a wooden bird.

These examples all happen to be similes. Point out the use of *like* and *as* to create the comparisons. When ready, move on the Activity #2

Activity #2

    Make three columns on the chalkboard labeling each one separately: simile, metaphor, and personification. Spend some time here instructing about the other two forms of figurative language. You could use specific examples from the following test, focusing on the ones from earlier chapters. Perhaps you could cite some examples from familiar songs. Ask why they think any author or lyricist would use them? Do they use them? Why? In what way does using them enhance speaking or writing or the understanding of each of these. As a whole group, have students give you examples they can think of and then have them locate a few in any part of the text they have read. Allow them to come to the board and write these under the correct heading. When you are satisfied with their ability to recognize them and differentiate between them, go to the next activity.

Activity #3

    Divide the class into small groups of three or four. Have each group assign a recorder. Give them a couple of sheets of paper. Ask each group to locate as many of these figures of speech as they can from the text. They may be more successful in the portion they already have read, but it isn't necessary to limit them. Giving them a time constraint is an option. It could be a race, you are the judge. You may want to rule out using the ones that are posted on the board. It's up to you. There are an endless supply in every chapter. Wrap this activity up by having the group with the **most** read their

(Lesson Eight Continued)

list aloud. Decide as a whole group if indeed each one is correct. Have all groups check off the ones that are read that they also found. Allow every group to read any that have not yet been mentioned. You could give small treats for first, second, third place, etc.

Activity #4

Have students create one example of each type. They could be individual sentences or you could require them to write a short paragraph using all three. Base this on the ability level of your students and/or time. Create one together as a model. If time, have them illustrate it with original art work or magazine pictures. Save finished products for display. They could do this part as homework.

NOTE: The following figurative language test is optional. You may want to use it right after instruction, later in this unit, or not at all. You may choose to use it only as a resource for this lesson. It contains examples from the entire book.

FIGURATIVE LANGUAGE TEST - *The Slave Dancer*

I. Read the following examples of figurative language. Label each one separately with either an **S** for simile, **P** for personification, or an **M** for metaphor. **BONUS:** Circle the *six* that can be more than one type.

1. I imagined the yellow stuff to be a kind of sweat thrown off by the Mississippi River. _____
2. "Oh, swim!" I would cry as if I could make the river return my father to us._____
3. At first the wind had been a tight fist, but now it was an open hand pushing us before it at such a rousing clip I felt my own arms had become wings as we flew across the water.._____
4. Then, as if daylight was being born inside the boat itself, I began to make out piles of rope.____
5. Purvis became a stone. _____
6. "I'm as neat as a pin, stack them up like flannel cakes, one on top of the other." _____
7. The sun began to die on the horizon, and still he beat him._____
8. Spark stalked about the ship like a spirit of mold and decay. _____
9. The egg was as luminous as a tiny moon rising between deck and rail._____
10. "Africa is nothing but a bottomless sack of blacks."_____
11. Time hung on us._____
12. A great white moon hung poised above the mast, striping the deck with pale unearthly rays.___
13. The weak light from the oil lamp cast shadows shaped like spoons on the faces of the men.___
14. The men's ankles had been gnawed at by their shackles as if they were alive and vicious. _____
15. Ned became thinner as though his substance was leaking away through his hammock._____
16. I was a stone cast into a stream, making circles that widened to the limits of the space._____
17. I saw hundreds of great white maggots with crescent mouths upon which were stitched horrible teeth. "Sharks," said Cooley. "Snap us up like flies."_____
18. I sat down among them as if I had been dropped into the sea._____
19. We floated like a live ember in a great bowl of darkness._____
20. The slaves were like statues._____
21. I heard a moan, muffled like the cry of a sea bird in a heavy rain._____
22. Everything marched at dead measure. _____
23. I yearned to show him my resolve as though it were a thing like a shoe or hoe._____
24. Instead, at regular intervals as though they'd been embroidered, were the distinct shapes of horses' hooves._____
25. I bounded down the road like a rabbit that had regained control of its limbs._____
26. I felt the little house shake in all its boards and bricks. _____
27. Time softened my memory as though it was kneading wax._____
28. I would see once again as though they'd never ceased their dancing in my mind, black men and women and children lifting their tormented limbs in time to a reedy martial air, the dust rising from their joyless thumping, the sound of the fife finally drowned beneath the clanging of their chains._____

II. List one example of your own for each type of figurative language. They can be original or from your favorite songs or poetry.

ANSWER KEY: FIGURATIVE LANGUAGE TEST - *The Slave Dancer*

I.
1. P
2. S
3. M, P
4. S, P
5. M
6. S
7. P
8. S
9. S
10. M
11. P
12. P
13. S
14. S, M
15. S
16. M
17. M, S
18. S
19. S
20. S
21. S
22. P
23. S
24. S
25. S
26. P
27. P, S
28. S, P

LESSON TEN

Objectives
1. To give students practice in reading orally
2. To evaluate students' oral reading

Activity #1

Have students read "Nicholas Spark Walks On Water" orally in class. You probably know the best way to get readers within your class; pick students at random, ask for volunteers, have students who have just read select another student, assign numbers to students and spin a spinner, or whatever works best for you. Complete the oral reading evaluation form that follows this lesson after listening to your students read.

ORAL READING EVALUATION - *The Slave Dancer*

Name _____ Class____ Date _____

SKILL	EXCELLENT	GOOD	AVERAGE	FAIR	POOR
Fluency	5	4	3	2	1
Clarity	5	4	3	2	1
Audibility	5	4	3	2	1
Pronunciation	5	4	3	2	1
_____	5	4	3	2	1
_____	5	4	3	2	1

Total _____ Grade _____

Comments:

LESSON ELEVEN

Objective
1. To review vocabulary and main ideas and events from "Nicholas Spark Walks On Water"
2. To give students practice in writing to persuade

Activity #1

Duplicate the matching section of the vocabulary page from "The Spaniard." Have students number to eight and fill in what they think are the correct answers. Now, use the multiple choice study guide questions from "The Spaniard" as a quiz to test students' reading of assigned text and as a review of the main ideas.(Use same paper as for above quiz) Exchange papers to check. Discuss answers to insure understanding. Encourage note taking for their later study use.

Activity #2

Assign PVR for "The Spaniard" as homework to be completed by the next class session.

Activity #3

Distribute Writing Assignment #2 and discuss the directions in detail. Allow the remaining class time for students to complete the assignment. Give them specifics of when final copies are due to you.

WRITING ASSIGNMENT #2 - *The Slave Dancer*

PROMPT

You have been exposed to many of the horrors of slave trading in your reading of the first five chapters of *The Slave Dancer*. The misfortunes imbedded within this tragic operation are countless.

In this writing assignment, pretend you are a United States' citizen living in the 1840's. You are violently opposed to slave trading and your objective is to persuade slaveowners to stop engaging in this barbaric practice. Be sure to use the authentic knowledge you have gained from the research the author did for this novel.

PREWRITING

To begin with, gather support for your viewpoint. Create a list of facts, opinions, and examples that support your point of view. Come up with any and all possible arguments you can think of that will promote your side of this issue. Decide which are your strongest justifiable arguments, and which are less substantial. Organize your points from weaker to strongest utilizing your facts, opinions, and examples as evidence in support of your argument.

DRAFTING

Begin with an introductory paragraph in which you express your outrage with all aspects of the dehumanizing practice of slave trading. Follow that with one paragraph for each of the main points you have to support your argument to convince slave owners to stop slave trading. Fill in each paragraph with your facts, opinions, and examples that support your main point. Then, write an ending paragraph that summarizes and restates your opposition to this practice as your final statement.

PROMPT

When you finish the rough draft of your paper, ask a student who sits near you to read it. After reading your rough draft, he\she should tell you what he\she liked best about your work, which parts were difficult to understand, and ways in which your work could be improved. Reread your paper considering your critic's comments, and make the corrections you think are necessary.

PROOFREADING

Do a final proofreading of your paper double-checking your grammar, spelling, organization, and the clarity of your ideas.

LESSON TWELVE

Objectives
    1. To review the vocabulary and main ideas and events from" The Spaniard"
    2. To discuss the theme of cruelty
    3. To discuss PROJECT MULTICULTURAL AWARENESS, a project that accompanies this unit
    4. To preview the study guide questions for "Ben Stout Makes A Mistake"
    5. To practice making predictions

Activity #1

    Divide the class into two teams. Play a game like a spelling bee, but instead of spelling a word, they must answer one of the study guide questions correctly or give an acceptable definition for vocabulary word. Using the study guide questions and matching vocabulary list from "The Spaniard", begin play. 1. Determine which team goes first. 2. Read one of the questions or give one of the vocabulary words for one team member to answer. 3. If it was answered correctly, that team gets a point. 4. If it was not answered correctly, the other team gets a try at the same question. 5. Question goes back and forth until it is answered correctly. 6. Read another question, and repeat earlier play. 7. Continue play until all questions and vocabulary on "The Spaniard" have been covered. 8. Reward winning team with some small prize or other incentive.

Activity #2

    Have students define the word cruelty. Write it and their input on the board or overhead. Then have them cite examples of cruelty from the story thus far. This could be done as a class, or in small groups or partners. Explore to whom the acts of cruelty are especially directed. This is a good place to delve into racial/cultural discrimination. Discuss the various effects of cruelty (low self-worth, violence, mental illness, etc.) Develop the opinion that those treated cruelly, often behave likewise. Ask if they know of instances where this cause and effect pattern exists (i.e. child abuse, domestic violence, alcoholism). This could act as a lead- in for an explanation of the following optional project, if you choose to use it as part of this unit.

Activity #3

    Have students skim study guide questions for "Ben Stout's Mistake". After skimming, have students pair up and predict the answers to these questions. Each partner does half of the questions. Ask students to put these predictions away for later reference. Assign the prereading vocabulary work and reading for "Ben Stout's Mistake" for the next class session. Begin in class, if time allows.

PROJECT MULTICULTURAL AWARENESS

Objectives:

Project Multicultural Awareness is a total class project for use in conjunction with this novel. *The Slave Dancer* is an unnerving narrative of slaving practices involving disturbing mistreatment of black Africans. It would be very hard not to raise the issue of racial and cultural discrimination and prejudice during or after the reading of it. For this reason, it seems an ideal occasion to challenge students with the task of learning more about their own racial and cultural heritage, as well as those of their classmates and community. Hopefully, the results of this project will not only create an awareness of cultural differences, but help to, through education, generate acceptance and tolerance. This novel and project can be taught at any time during the calendar year, although tying it into a Martin Luther King Day celebration, or Black History Month, or any other ethnic unit may enhance it even further.

THE PROJECT

This project is separate from the rest of *The Slave Dancer* unit, so you can either use it while you are doing the *Slave Dancer* unit or as a separate mini-unit after you have completed the unit test for the book. Also, having it as a separate project enables you to eliminate it if you want to or need to for some reason, without disrupting the normal flow of the unit.

Assignment 1 Divide your class into small groups of three or four. Provide students with a large piece of unlined paper. Together, ask the group of students to make a basic sketch of their impression of a map of the world, including all seven continents. Accuracy is not the important issue. Show them a world map or globe briefly, if they are very worried about exactness. After they have completed this, ask each member to place their initials or name on any location to which they feel a connection. This could be where their ancestors originated, where their name came from, etc. Once this portion of the activity is over in their small groups, return to the large class group. Chart on one world map, the results of the small group activity. Encourage those students who were unaware of any part of their heritage to try to discover some information before the next class session.

Assignment 2 Create a list of various ethnic/cultural groups represented by you and your class. Develop groups based on the different representations. Ask the class if they feel there are any ethnic/cultural groups not represented by you or the class. If so, ask for volunteers from the class (especially from some larger similar background group) to represent those groups. Inform students that their objective is to become an expert on this ethnic/cultural group. Have them brainstorm ideas for topics they think would be appropriate for an expert to know about. (For example: history, language, holidays, celebrations, dress, societal accomplishments by group members, food, music, religion, gender roles, etc.) Guide them in developing these topics for research.

The Slave Dancer project Page 2

    <u>Assignment 3</u> It is now time for each group to research their cultural/ethnic group. Allow students to devise their own plan for obtaining the information they need. Some possible directions might include: use of the library, interviewing people, inviting speakers, watching films, use of computer software, off campus visits, etc. At this point, set up a timetable for finalizing this portion of the project. It may be helpful for you to assign various responsibilities per group, or allow each group to determine their own responsible parties who will report to you. Inspiration and motivation for this portion of the project can be done by relaying to the class that they will be creatively presenting the results of their research (heritage festival/fair or your plan) as the culmination of this project. Encourage organized compilation of this important data through the use of charts, notebooks, note cards, files, or whatever else would be appropriate for your students.

    <u>Assignment 4</u> Once the information from the previous assignment is collected, groups need to determine how they would like to best present their findings to the rest of the school, grade, or community. This feature of the project will be determined by your level of commitment to it and your resources. Any number of possibilities would work here. Staging a festival with music, food, and other authentic information- sharing would be the ideal. Including adult community members and class relatives provide valuable life skills in communication and generation-bridging. Although this project may sound very time consuming or immense, the benefits of affording this opportunity for your class could be staggering.

LESSON THIRTEEN

Objectives
    1. To practice vocabulary from "Ben Stout's Mistake"
    2. To review the main ideas and events from "Ben Stout's Mistake"
    3. To do the prereading vocabulary work for "The Old Man; Home and After"
    4. To preview study guide questions for "The Old Man ; Home and After"

Activity #1

    Have students glance over the vocabulary from "Ben Stout's Mistake." Write each of the twelve words separately on the chalkboard leaving space beneath each one, or on separate pieces of newsprint taped to the wall around the room. Divide the class into twelve teams or pairs.. Have each team list as many synonyms for their word as they can come up with, beneath it, on the chalkboard or newsprint. Give them a time limit and reward the team who comes up with the most correct synonyms. It is up to you if you want them to be able to refer to a thesaurus or dictionary first. If class can handle, you could have them give an at least one antonym for their word too.

Activity #2

    Review the main ideas and events from "Ben Stout's Mistake" allowing your class to decide in which manner they would like to do that. They could choose from any of the earlier techniques, or devise a new one. Have them retrieve their predictions from Lesson Eleven and determine how well they did. Perhaps give some special privilege to the partners who were the most accurate.

Activity #3

    Have students preview the study guide questions and prereading vocabulary work for "The Old Man; Home and After" independently or for homework.

LESSON FOURTEEN

Objectives:
1. To review vocabulary from "The Old Man; Home and After"
2. To practice reading orally
3. To reinforce the main ideas and events from "The Old Man; Home and After"
4. To practice characterization

Activity #1
    Pair students up. Using their vocabulary sheets from these chapters, have one partner act out a word, while the other partner tries to guess which word it is. Alternate play until all words have been covered. This is similar to the game Charades.

Activity #2
    Have students read the final two chapters orally. Refer to Lesson Nine for ideas on motivation.

Activity #3
    Reinforce the main ideas and events of these chapters using the multiple choice study guide questions as a quiz. Have students exchange papers to grade. Be sure they take notes for future reference.

Activity #4
    Hand out table character charts for Ras, young slave and Daniel, older escaped slave. Work together to fill these out or assign as homework, if time is limited.

LESSON FIFTEEN

Objective:
    To give students practice in writing to express personal ideas

Activity
    Distribute directions for Writing Assignment #3. Discuss in great detail. Allow students the remainder of the class period to work on this assignment.

WRITING ASSIGNMENT #3 - *The Slave Dancer*

PROMPT

You have learned that this experience affected Jessie in many ways. Perhaps the most profound effect was one that did not yield to time. He was unable to ever listen to music again. He says he could not bear to hear a woman sing, and at the sound of any instrument: a fiddle, a flute, a drum, or a comb with paper wrapped around it played by his child, he would leave instantly and shut himself away.

Your assignment is to share music's influence in your life.

PREWRITING

The first thing you need to consider are the emotions music causes you to feel. When do you listen to music? What is your favorite type of music, least favorite? Do different kinds of music cause different reactions in you? Can music be healing? destructive? How would your life change without any music whatsoever? Jot down your thoughts, feelings, and opinions on these questions and any other ideas you may have.

DRAFTING

Begin your paper with an introductory paragraph giving your audience an indication of the role music plays in your life. This paragraph's purpose is to lead into the body of your composition, which is coming next.

The body of your composition should contain the information generated from your thoughts and responses to the questions in the prewriting section. Begin with one set of feelings, thoughts, and responses you came up with for one of the questions. Continue until you have covered each of them adequately.

Finish your composition with a concluding paragraph in which you express your final statements about the role music plays in your world.

PROMPT

When you finish your rough draft, ask a student who sits near you to read it. After reading your rough draft, he/she should tell you what he/she liked best about your work, which parts were difficult to understand, and ways in which your work could be improved. Reread your paper considering your critic's comments and make the corrections you think are necessary.

PROOFREADING

Do a final proofreading of your paper double-checking your grammar, spelling, organization, and the clarity of your ideas.

LESSONS SIXTEEN AND SEVENTEEN

Objectives:
1. To discuss the ideas and themes from *The Slave Dancer* in greater detail
2. To have students exercise their interpretive and critical thinking skills
3. To relate some of the ideas in *The Slave Dancer* to the students' lives
4. To give students the opportunity to share any extra activities or writing assignments they have completed

Activity #1

Choose the questions from the Extra Discussion Questions/Writing Assignments which seem most appropriate for your students. A class discussion of these questions is most effective if students have been given the opportunity to formulate answers to the questions prior to the discussion. To this end, you may either have all the students formulate answers to all the questions, divide your class into groups and assign one or more questions to each group, or you could assign one question to each student in your class. The option you choose will make a difference in the amount of class time needed for this activity.

Activity #2

After students have had ample time to formulate answers to the questions, begin your class discussion of the questions and the ideas presented by the questions. Be sure students take notes during the discussion so they have information to study for the unit test.

Activity #3

Give those students who have completed any extra activities related to this unit the opportunity to share now. If students would like to share their writing assignments, do this now. Perhaps they could share a music sample for the writing to express personal ideas.

EXTRA DISCUSSION QUESTIONS/WRITING ASSIGNMENTS
The Slave Dancer

Interpretive

1. From what point of view is the story written? How does it affect us as we read it?

2. Identify the setting and tell how it shapes this story.

3. What are the main conflicts in the story and how are they resolved?

4. What is foreshadowing? Give examples of foreshadowing used in *The Slave Dancer*.

5. Using your completed character charts, write a character sketch for two characters of your choice. From your listed details, classify and summarize their traits determining their personality.

6. How were the black slaves portrayed by the author?

7. Define climax. Next, summarize the main events leading up to **it** and the remaining events after **it** that create the resolution.

8. How did Paula Fox's research enable her to create such a horrifying tale?

9. Purvis is a firm slaver in most ways, seeming to believe in his mission. What surprising statement of his on page 92 indicates he may be capable of a different perspective?

Critical

10. What did the small and isolated island Jessie spotted near Cuban waters represent to him?

11. Explain the significance of the ship's name, *The Moonlight*.

12. How did the slaves in the hold treat Jessie when Stout lowered him down into the hold to retrieve his fife? Why do you think they behaved in this manner?

13. Compare and contrast Jessie's life in New Orleans with his life on *The Moonlight*.

14. What does the New Orleans' slave woman "Star" represent to Jessie?

15. How would the story have changed if Ras and Jessie had not been helped by Daniel?

16. Why did the crew of *The Moonlight* tolerate the Captain's abuse, the exhausting work, and the horrible conditions?

The Slave Dancer Extra Discussion Questions page 2

17. Contrast Aunt Agatha's behavior and personality *before* and *after* Jessie's kidnapping.

18. Explain what Purvis was referring to when he told Jessie they'd have a ship full of *royalty* for him to play for.

19. Reveal the contradiction within Wick's statement to Cooley," Leave off with your birds! It's only savages who'd take pleasure in such a spectacle."

20. Why do you think the author based the story on a *shipwrecked* slave ship? What does the shipwreck symbolize?

21. Explain Jessie's statement upon returning to New Orleans, "I made a promise to myself: I would do nothing that was connected ever so faintly with the importing and sale and use of slaves. But I soon discovered that everything I considered bore, somewhere along the way, the imprint of black hands."

Critical/ Personal Response
22. Was there anything Jessie could have done to stop the cruelty on the ship? He did refuse to play his flute at one point, knowing he would suffer consequences. How would you have reacted to what he witnessed? Have you ever acted on your conscience despite probable punishment?

23. Why does Ned ask Jessie, "Haven't you heard of the wages of sin? Did you think they were gold?" What do **you** think are the "wages of sin"?

24. Are Jessie and Ras compatible? How? In what ways are you compatible with your friends?

25. Do you think Jessie comes to better terms with his father's fate due to this ordeal? What experience of yours has given you insight into a previous event?

26. What does Jessie learn about himself through this incident? How do you think it helped him in Andersonville? Have you ever experienced something unpleasant that caused you to learn more about yourself?

27. What was Purvis saying to Stout when he told him,"we'll be on land again where men is the same height" ? How is this statement related to power? How did the Captain and First Mates exercise their command on *The Moonlight*? Have you ever been the victim of ill-use of power?

28. Have you read any other books written by Paula Fox? How do they compare to *The Slave Dancer*? Which one is your favorite? Why?

The Slave Dancer Extra Discussion Questions page 3

Personal Response

29. Describe how you would have felt if the only grown people you had known were primarily women and suddenly you were thrown into an environment of only men, the likes of those on *The Moonlight*.

30. Jessie became fond of and trusted Purvis, even though he was rough on him. Can you relate to this? Have you ever had a similar relationship?

31. Slavery evokes strong feelings of racial discrimination Share a time you or someone you know felt discriminated against. Why did you feel you were treated differently and how did you respond?

32. If you had been living during this time period, would you have been involved in slave trading? Why or why not?

Quotations

1. "Go and borrow some candles from Aunt Agatha. I must start on this nightmare right away."

2. "Don't walk there! Can't you walk like a gentleman instead of a bayou lout?"

3. "What an undignified way to earn your keep! Playing that silly pipe! It's time you were apprenticed and learned a trade. I doubt you'd benefit from schooling."

4. "Take up that pipe, Claudius. He's worth nothing without his pipe."

5. "Don't you remember a man who gave you money? I'm about to do even more for you. I'm going to take you on a fine sea voyage."

6. "My mother will think I'm dead!."

7. "I'm only a carpenter. You might as well settle yourself to what's happened. The Captain will have what he will have no matter how he gets it."

8. "No, no. Not playing for the Captain, but for kings and princes and other such like trash. Why, we'll have a ship full of royalty, won't we?"

9. "I won't have Ibos. They're soft as melons and kill themselves if they're not watched twenty-four hours a day. I will not put up with such creatures!"

The Slave Dancer Extra Discussion Questions page 4

10. "I'd never thought a cockroach was a sea-going creature. I didn't care for the breed. Still, I found it a touch comforting that such a familiar land thing was making itself at home on me."

11. "They've different laws than us. They've entirely stopped the slave trade in their own country- the worse for them- and would like us to copy them in their folly. Why, the trade is the best trade there is! Black Gold, we call it! Still, there's the one way they help us. The native chiefs are so greedy for our trade goods, they sell their people cheaper that they ever did to tempt us to run the British blockade. So we profit despite the damned Englishmen."

12. "That's where the slaves will be stowed, right on those casks, and in the aft hold when we've unloaded the rum."

13. "Yes. I'm a tight packer, as neat as a pin, stack them up like flannel cakes, one on top of the other. Ah- it's the British who've forced me to be so ingenious."

14. "Don't forget Jonah and what happened to him, only you shall land up in the belly of a shark."

15. "There would've been no use in that. The officers of this ship would not care what the truth was. The Captain had it in his mind that it was time for a flogging-to remind the men."

16. "It's this way. If an American patrol should signal us and demand to board the ship, we'd run up a Spanish flag. And if they persisted, we'd show them a full set of papers that would prove *The Moonlight* to be of Spanish ownership."

17. "All of Africa is nothing but a bottomless sack of blacks."

18. "You dance them because it keeps them healthy. It's hard to make a profit out of a sick nigger- the insurance ain't so easy to collect."

19. "The African was tempted and then became depraved by a desire for the material things offered him by debased traders. It's all the Devil's work."

20. "I hated the slaves! I hated their shuffling, their howling, their very suffering!"

21. "You're not so young you don't know what an order is."

22. "I have a touch of death. Haven't you heard of the wages of sin? Did you think they were gold?"

The Slave Dancer Extra Discussion Questions page 5

23. "It's not because he pointed his pistol at him. Old Cawthorne's been through mutinies before. He never lost a hair! But Cawthorne knew the black would recover-they can survive floggings that would kill a white man a hundred times over- and Spark killed him. Don't you see? *There went the profit*!

24. "Cooley, leave off with your birds! It's only savages who'd take pleasure in such a spectacle. We've outlawed it in Massachusetts."

25. "I've been good to you. I don't understand your ingratitude. They've all talked against me. I suppose that accounts for it."

26. "There's someone makes little dolls of him and sprinkles them with gunpowder and steals along the docks and places a doll in each ship- and when it's out at sea, the doll grows and grows till it looks just like another sailor man, and it takes its place among the crew and no one's the wiser until two weeks at sea when one of the crew says to another, 'Ain't he dead? That one over there by the helm?' and the other one says,' Just what I was thinking- we've got a dead man on the ship-'"

27. "I'll never ship on a slaver again." "Never, Jessie! You see if I don't keep my word!"

28. "Yes, I think it's in one of the holds. That's what I think. Someone has taken it and dropped it down to the niggers so's they can play their own tunes. Go down there and fetch it up. You're sure to find it there."

29. "Sharks. Snap us up like flies."

30. "We'll be in Cuban waters in a day or so, and not long after that, we'll be on land again where men is the same height. "

31. "But Cawthorne's so greedy- he's like a man choking on one chicken bone while he's grabbing for another."

32. "A sister, older than me. That's all. She lives in Boston or used to. I haven't seen her in fifteen years. She's dead for all I know. My home is where I'm at."

33. "A miracle!"

34. "If they are dead they are of no use to me! "

The Slave Dancer Extra Discussion Questions page 6

35. "By God! I see the ship! I see it. *It's American*! You disaster, Stout! You've murdered me! Get the slaves over! Get them over!"

36. "Even now I can feel the urgency of our struggle, the hope that delivered me from the depths and brought me up to air again and again as though most of my true life had taken place in that stretch of sea."

37. "Oh, swim!"

38. "You won't find nobody. The sharks will crack their bones."

39. "We're going to get him out of here. We got a way of taking him north, far from this place."

40. "Jessie? Nose. Teef. Jessie."

41. "If you tell your people about Daniel, Daniel be taken back to the place he run away from."

42. "I can't hear it! I can't bear it!"

43. "At first I made a promise to myself: I would do nothing that was connected ever so faintly with the importing and sale and use of slaves. But I soon discovered that everything I considered bore, somewhere along the way, the imprint of black hands."

44. "For at the first note of a tune or a song, I would see once again as though they'd never ceased their dancing in my mind, black men and women and children lifting their tormented limbs to a reedy martial air, the dust rising from their joyless thumping, the sound of the fife finally drowned beneath the clanging of their chains."

LESSON EIGHTEEN

Objectives
>   To review all of the vocabulary work done in this unit

Activity
>   Choose one (or more) of the vocabulary review activities listed below and spend your class period as directed in the activity. Some of the materials for these review activities are located in the Unit Resource section of this unit.

Vocabulary Review Activities

1. Divide your class into two teams and have an old-fashioned spelling or definition bee.
2. Give each of your students (or students in groups of two, three or four) a *The Slave Dancer* Vocabulary Word Search Puzzle. The person (group) to find all of the vocabulary words in the puzzle first wins.
3. Give students a *The Slave Dancer* Vocabulary Word Search Puzzle without the word list. The person or group to find the most vocabulary words in the puzzle wins.
4. Use a *The Slave Dancer* Vocabulary Crossword Puzzle. Put the puzzle onto a transparency on the overhead projector (so everyone can see it), and do the puzzle together as a class.
5. Give students a *The Slave Dancer* Vocabulary Matching Worksheet to do.
6. Divide your class into two teams. Use *The Slave Dancer* vocabulary words with their letters jumbled as a word list. Student 1 from Team A faces off against Student 1 from Team B. You write the first jumbled word on the board. The first student (1A or 1B) to unscramble the word wins the chance for his/her team to score points. If 1A wins the jumble, go to student 2A and give him/her a definition. He/she must give you the correct spelling of the vocabulary word which fits that definition. If he/she does, Team A scores a point, and you give student 3A a definition for which you expect a correctly spelled matching vocabulary word. Continue giving Team A definitions until some team member makes an incorrect response. An incorrect response sends the game back to the jumbled-word face off, this time with students 2A and 2B. Instead of repeating giving definitions to the first few students of each team, continue with the student after the one who gave the last incorrect response on the team. For example, if Team B wins the jumbled-word face-off, and student 5B gave the last incorrect answer for Team B, you would start this round of definition questions with student 6B, and so on. The team with the most points wins!
7. Have students write a story in which they correctly use as many vocabulary words as possible. Have students read their compositions orally. Post the most original compositions on your bulletin board.

LESSON NINETEEN

Objective
 To review the main ideas presented in *The Slave Dancer*

Activity #1
 Choose one of the review games/activities included in the packet and spend your class period as outlined there. Some materials for these activities are located in the Extra Activities Packet section of this unit.

Activity #2
 Remind students that the Unit Test will be in the next class meeting. Stress the review of the Study Guides and their class notes as a last minute, brush-up review for the unit test.

REVIEW GAMES/ACTIVITIES - *The Slave Dancer*

1. Ask the class to make up a unit test for *The Slave Dancer*. The test should have 4 sections: matching, true/false, short answer, and essay. Students may use 1/2 period to make the test and then swap papers and use the other 1/2 class period to take a test a classmate has devised. (open book) You may want to use the unit test included in this packet or take questions from the students' unit tests to formulate your own test.

2. Take 1/2 period for students to make up true and false questions (including the answers). Collect the papers and divide the class into two teams. Draw a big tic-tac-toe board on the chalk board. Make one team X and one team O. Ask questions to each side, giving each student one turn. If the question is answered correctly, that students' team's letter (X or O) is placed in the box. If the answer is incorrect, no mark is placed in the box. The object is to get three marks in a row like tic-tac-toe. You may want to keep track of the number of games won for each team.

3. Take 1/2 period for students to make up questions (true/false and short answer). Collect the questions. Divide the class into two teams. You'll alternate asking questions to individual members of teams A & B (like in a spelling bee). The question keeps going from A to B until it is correctly answered, then a new question is asked. A correct answer does not allow the team to get another question. Correct answers are +2 points; incorrect answers are -1 point.

4. Have students pair up and quiz each other from their study guides and class notes.

5. Give students a *The Slave Dancer* crossword puzzle to complete.

6. Divide your class into two teams. Use *The Slave Dancer* crossword words with their letters jumbled as a word list. Student 1 from Team A faces off against Student 1 from Team B. You write the first jumbled word on the board. The first student (1A or 1B) to unscramble the word wins the chance for his/her team to score points. If 1A wins the jumble, go to student 2A and give him/her a clue. He/she must give you the correct word which matches that clue. If he/she does, Team A scores a point, and you give student 3A a clue for which you expect another correct response. Continue giving Team A clues until some team member makes an incorrect response. An incorrect response sends the game back to the jumbled-word face off, this time with students 2A and 2B. Instead of repeating giving clues to the first few students of each team, continue with the student after the one who gave the last incorrect response on the team. For example, if Team B wins the jumbled-word face-off, and student 5B gave the last incorrect answer for Team B, you would start this round of clue questions with student 6B, and so on.

UNIT TESTS

SHORT ANSWER UNIT TEST #1 - *The Slave Dancer*

I. Matching/Identify

___ Bollweevil   A. Englishmen trying to stop slave trade

___ The Moonlight   B. Used to try to clear stench from the holds

___ chloride of lime   C. Kidnapped New Orleans' boy

___ thirteen   D. Slaving ship

___ pressed   E. Corner of St. Louis and Chartres Streets

___ Daniel   F. Purvis and Mary played this with Jessie

___ cat's cradle   G. Slave trade

___ slave market   H. Captain's nickname for Jessie

___ bayou lout   I. Aunt Agatha's name for Jessie

___ British Blockade   J. Jessie did this under an apothecary

___ Black Gold   K. Slave dancer's age

___ Purvis   L. Pressganged or forced into ship's service

___ Jessie   M. Ropes that support the mast

___ apprentice   N. Kidnapper Jessie came to trust

___ shrouds   O. Old black Mississippian man

The Slave Dancer Short Answer Unit Test 1 Page 2

II. Short Answer

1. On his way from Aunt Agatha's, what happened to Jessie?

2. Where did his kidnappers deposit him?

3. Why was Jessie needed by these men?

4. Why was slave trading hazardous?

5. Describe the changes on the ship once it had becalmed.

6. For what reason was one of the crew members flogged?

7. How did slaving ships use different flags to their advantage?

8. How did Jessie's mood change upon seeing land?

9. What was Purvis 'response when Jessie criticized slaving?

The Slave Dancer Short Answer Unit Test 1 Page 3

10. Why did *The Moonlight* leave Whydah at night?

11. Which crew member admitted to the evilness of slave trading?

12. What realization of Jessie's caused him to defy his orders to play his fife?

13. How was Jessie able to temporarily escape the horrors of the ship?

14. Describe Purvis' characterization of Stout to Jessie.

15. Where did Jessie vow never to visit again if he made it home?

16. What is in the chest Jessie fetched from the Captain and what was its purpose?

17. Why did the Captain order the slaves overboard?

18. What words did Jessie say to himself while dogpawing from the ship to shore?

19. Where did Ras go?

20. Name the most long-lasting effect of Jessie's ordeal.

The Slave Dancer Short Answer Unit Test 1 page 4

III. Essay

    Reveal the contradiction within Wick's statement to Cooley, "Leave off with your birds! It's only savages who'd take pleasure in such a spectacle."

IV. Vocabulary

Listen to the vocabulary words and spell them. After you have spelled all the words, go back and write down the definitions.

1.

2.

3.

4.

5.

6.

7.

8.

9.

10.

KEY: SHORT ANSWER UNIT TEST #1 - *The Slave Dancer*

I. Matching/Identify

__H__ Bollweevil		A. Englishmen trying to stop slave trade
__D__ The Moonlight		B. Used to try to clear stench from the holds
__B__ chloride of lime		C. Kidnapped New Orleans' boy
__K__ thirteen		D. Slaving ship
__L__ pressed		E. Corner of St. Louis and Chartres Streets
__O__ Daniel		F. Purvis and Mary played this with Jessie
__F__ cat's cradle		G. Slave trade
__E__ slave market		H. Captain's nickname for Jessie
__I__ bayou lout		I. Aunt Agatha's name for Jessie
__A__ British Blockade		J. Jessie did this under an apothecary
__G__ Black Gold		K. Slave dancer's age
__N__ Purvis		L. Pressganged or forced into ship's service
__C__ Jessie		M. Ropes that support the mast
__J__ apprentice		N. Kidnapper Jessie came to trust
__M__ shrouds		O. Old black Mississippian man

II. Short Answer

1. On his way from Aunt Agatha's, what happened to Jessie?
    Two men cover him with canvas, forcing him to the ground. They carry him off as he passes out.

2. Where did his kidnappers deposit him?
    He is deposited on a slaving ship, *The Moonlight*.

3. Why was Jessie needed by these men?
    He was needed to play his fife to exercise(dance) the slaves.

4. Why was slave trading hazardous?
    There were groups of ships (U.S. Revenue Cutters and the British Blockaders trying to stop this practice. The weather conditions and ship conditions made it treacherous, as well.

5. Describe the changes on the ship once it had becalmed.
    Gratings had replaced the solid hatches over the holds, a huge cauldron appeared in Curry's galley, and Cooley was making a whip. Crew members' tempers were raging.

6. For what reason was one of the crew members flogged?
    Someone stole an egg from the Captain's quarters.

7. How did slaving ships use different flags to their advantage?
    The Captain kept more than one country's flag in his quarters. If the ship was stopped, he would run up another county's flag and bring out papers to prove ownership to the flag's country. Other counties' ships would do the same.

8. How did Jessie's mood change upon seeing land?
    He goes into a dark mood and sulks terribly. It bothers him to be so near land and not be able to get off.

9. What was Purvis' response when Jessie criticized slaving?
    He compares these circumstances with those of his ancestors who came over from Ireland sixty years earlier locked in a hold and sold.

10. Why did *The Moonlight* leave Wydah at night?
    So the slaves would not see the shore of their homeland disappearing.

11. Which crew member admits to the evilness of slave trading?
    Ned admits it's all the Devil's work.

12. What realization of Jessie's caused him to defy his orders to play his fife?
    He thinks he hates the slaves. Not to hear them! Not to smell them! Not to know of their existence!

13. How was Jessie able to temporarily escape the horrors of the ship?
    He found some freedom in his mind by imagining he was in another place- home. He would recall every object in his room on Pirate's Alley.

14. Describe Purvis' characterization of Stout to Jessie.
    Purvis says he is dead, that someone makes little dolls of him and sprinkles them with gunpowder and places one in every ship- and out at sea the doll grows till it looks like a sailor.

15. Where does Jessie vow never to visit again if he ever makes it home?
    He says he will never again go to the slave market in New Orleans.

16. What is in the chest Jessie fetched from the Captain and what was its purpose?
    There are fancy clothes for the slaves to dress up in on their last night on board.

17. Why did the Captain order the slaves overboard?
    The Spaniard's slave spotted an overtaking American ship and its convoy.

18. What words did Jessie say to himself while dogpawing from the ship to shore?
    "Oh, swim!"

19. Where did Ras go?
    He was taken north by some black men.

20. Name the most long-lasting effect of Jessie's ordeal.
    He was unable to listen to any kind of music ever again.

IV. Vocabulary
    Choose ten of the vocabulary words to read orally for the vocabulary section of this unit test.

SHORT ANSWER UNIT TEST 2 - *The Slave Dancer*

I. Matching/Identify

____ Daniel   A. Englishmen trying to stop slave trade

____ slave market   B. Used to try to clear stench from the holds

____ bayou lout   C. Kidnapped New Orleans' boy

____ cat's cradle   D. Slaving ship

____ pressed   E. Corner of St. Louis and Chartres Streets

____ Bollweevil   F. Purvis and Mary played this with Jessie

____ Purvis   G. Slave trade

____ thirteen   H. Captain's nickname for Jessie

____ chloride of lime   I. Aunt Agatha's name for Jessie

____ shrouds   J. Jessie did this under an apothecary

____ Jessie   K. Slave dancer's age

____ The Moonlight   L. Pressganged or forced into ship's service

____ Black Gold   M. Ropes that support the mast

____ apprentice   N. Kidnapper Jessie came to trust

____ British Blockade   O. Old black Mississippian man

The Slave Dancer Short Answer Unit Test 2 Page 2

II. Short Answer

1. How does Jessie's mother support her family?

2. How and when did Jessie's father die?

3. What does Jessie remember while walking by the walled gardens of the rich families?

4. Where and when had Jessie seen one of his kidnappers before?

5. What does the Captain exchange the slaves for in Africa?

6. Why do the British try to block the other slave trade

7. What jobs filled up Jessie's days on the ship?

The Slave Dancer Short Answer Unit Test 2 Page 3

8. What changes occurred on the ship once it had becalmed?

9. Who was wrongfully accused and punished by the Captain for stealing the egg?

10. How do slaving ships employ different flags to their advantage?

11. Why is it necessary for Jessie to play his fife for the slaves?

12. Upon seeing land, how does Jessie's mood change?

13. Jessie's comment about the kidnapping of the slaves causes Purvis to react in what way?

14. For what reason is Jessie smacked by Ned?

The Slave Dancer Short Answer Unit Test 2 Page 4

15. If the slaves will not dance, what happens to them?

16. What realization does Jessie have that causes him to defy his orders?

17. How is Jessie able to temporarily escape the horrors of the ship?

18. What revelation causes the Captain to order the slaves overboard?

19. What words does Jessie say to himself while dog pawing from the ship to the shore?

20. How does Jessie's mother handle his absence and return?

The Slave Dancer Short Answer Unit Test 2 Page 5

III. Quotations: Identify the speaker and explain the significance of these quotes:

1. "What an undignified way to earn your keep! Playing that silly pipe! It's time you were apprenticed and learned a trade. I doubt you'd benefit from schooling."

2. "Take up that pipe, Claudius. He's worth nothing without his pipe."

3. "No, no. Not playing for the Captain, but for kings and princes and other such like trash. Why, we'll have a ship full of royalty, won't we?"

4. "They've different laws than us. They've entirely stopped the slave trade in their own country- the worse for them- and would like us to copy them in their folly. Why, the trade is the best trade there is our trade goods, they sell their people cheaper that they ever did to tempt us to run the British blockade. So we profit despite the damned Englishmen."

5. "Yes. I'm a tight packer, as neat as a pin, stack them up like flannel cakes, one on top of the other. Ah- it's the British who've forced me to be so ingenious."

6. "All of Africa is nothing but a bottomless sack of blacks."

7. "The African was tempted and then became depraved by a desire for the material things offered him by debased traders. It's all the Devil's work."

8. "You're not so young you don't know what an order is."

The Slave Dancer Short Answer Unit Test 2 Page 6

9. The native chiefs are so greedy for our trade goods, they sell their people cheaper that they ever did to tempt us to run the British blockade. So we profit despite the damned Englishmen. "

10. "I have a touch of death. Haven't you heard of the wages of sin? Did you think they were gold?"

11. "It's not because he pointed his pistol at him. Old Cawthorne's been through mutinies before. He never lost a hair! But Cawthorne knew the black would recover-they can survive floggings that would kill a white man a hundred times over- and Spark killed him. Don't you see? *There went the profit*!

12. "There's someone makes little dolls of him and sprinkles them with gunpowder and steals along the docks and places a doll in each ship- and when it's out at sea, the doll grows and grows till it looks just like another sailor man, and it takes its place among the crew and no one's the wiser until two weeks at sea when one of the crew says to another, 'Ain't he dead? That one over there by the helm?' and the other one says,' Just what I was thinking- we've got a dead man on the ship-'"

13. "I'll never ship on a slaver again." "Never, Jessie! You see if I don't keep my word!"

14. "We'll be in Cuban waters in a day or so, and not long after that, we'll be on land again where men is the same height. "

The Slave Dancer Short Answer Unit Test 2 Page 7

15. "Even now I can feel the urgency of our struggle, the hope that delivered me from the depths and brought me up to air again and again as though most of my true life had taken place in that stretch of sea."

16. "Jessie? Nose. Teef. Jessie."

17. "I made a promise to myself: I would do nothing that was connected ever so faintly with the importing and sale and use of slaves. But I soon discovered that everything I considered bore, somewhere along the way, the imprint of black hands."

The Slave Dancer Short Answer Unit Test 2 page 8

Vocabulary

Listen to the vocabulary words and spell them. After you have spelled all the words, go back and write down the definitions.

1.

2.

3.

4.

5.

6.

7.

8.

9.

10.

KEY: SHORT ANSWER UNIT TEST 2 *The Slave Dancer*

I. Matching/Identify

__O__	Daniel	A. Englishmen trying to stop slave trade
__E__	slave market	B. Used to try to clear stench from the holds
__I__	bayou lout	C. Kidnapped New Orleans' boy
__F__	cat's cradle	D. Slaving ship
__L__	pressed	E. Corner of St. Louis and Chartres Streets
__H__	Bollweevil	F. Purvis and Mary played this with Jessie
__N__	Purvis	G. Slave trade
__K__	thirteen	H. Captain's nickname for Jessie
__B__	chloride of lime	I. Aunt Agatha's name for Jessie
__M__	shrouds	J. Jessie did this under an apothecary
__C__	Jessie	K. Slave dancer's age
__D__	The Moonlight	L. Pressganged or forced into ship's service
__G__	Black Gold	M. Ropes that support the mast
__J__	apprentice	N. Kidnapper Jessie came to trust
__A__	British Blockade	O. Old black Mississippian man

II. Short Answer

1. How did Jessie's mother support her family?
    Jessie's mother was a seamstress; making gowns for the rich ladies of New Orleans.

2. How and when did Jessie's father die?
    He drowned nine years earlier in the Mississippi River while working to clear it of tree stumps and other hidden debris for steamboat passage.

3. What does Jessie remember while walking by the walled gardens of the rich families?
    He recalls a slave woman watching him as he climbed the walls on e day to peek in. She was summoned back to the house by someone calling the name "Star'. He was fascinated by the name, and wondered what she thought of it.

4. Where and when had Jessie seen one of his kidnappers before?
    He was a rough-looking sailor who had given Jessie two pennies to play a martial tune on his fife earlier that same day, down by the fruit stalls by the river.

5. What does the Captain exchange the slaves for in Africa?
    He exchanges money ($10 a head), rum, and tobacco for the slaves.

6. Why did the British try to block the other slave traders?
    They had entirely stopped slave trading in their country and didn't want other countries continuing the practice.

7. What jobs filled up Jessie's days on the ship?
    He waited on the Captain, heaved waste over the side, mended sails, and chased rate

8. What changes occurred on the ship once it had becalmed?
    Gratings replaced the solid hatches over the holds, a huge cauldron appeared in Curry's galley, and Cooley was making a whip.

9. Who was wrongfully accused and punished by the Captain for stealing the egg?
    Purvis was flogged and tied to the shrouds.

10. How did slaving ships employ different flags to their advantage?
    Their Captains kept more than one country's flag in their quarters. If the ship was stopped, they would run up another country's flag and bring out papers to prove ownership to the flag's country.

11. Why is it necessary for Jessie to play his fife for the slaves?
    The slaves need music to dance to keep them healthy.

12. Upon seeing land, how does Jessie's mood change?
    He goes into a dark mood and sulks terribly. It bothers him to be so near land and not be able to get off.

13. Jessie's comment about the kidnapping of the slaves causes Purvis to react in what way?
    He compares these circumstances with those of his ancestors who came over4 from Ireland sixty years earlier locked in a hold and sold.

14. For what reason is Jessie smacked by Ned?
    When a little black girl was carried to the rail and flung into the water by Spark, Jessie cried out. Ned then smacked him.

15. If the slaves will not dance, what happens to them?
    They are whipped till they rise, or their bare feet stepped on with Spark's booted heel.

16. What realization does Jessie have that causes him to defy his orders to play his fife?
    He thinks he hates the slaves! Not to hear or smell them! Not know of their existence!

17. How is Jessie able to temporarily escape the horrors of the ship?
    He found some freedom in his mind by imaging he was in another place- home. He would recall every object in his room on Pirate's Alley.

18. What revelation causes the Captain to order the slaves overboard?
    The overtaking ship and its convoy is American.

19. What words does Jessie say to himself while dog pawing from the ship to the shore?
    He thinks of his drowned father and the words he wanted to tell him "Oh, swim!

20. How does Jessie's mother handle his absence and return?
    She questions the market venders daily about him, begins to think him dead, and is terrified of the story he tells and the fate of the slaves.

III. Quotations

IV. Vocabulary
    Choose ten of the vocabulary words to read orally for the vocabulary section of the test.

ADVANCED SHORT ANSWER UNIT TEST - *The Slave Dancer*

I. Matching

____ Daniel   A. Englishmen trying to stop slave trade

____ slave market   B. Used to try to clear stench from the holds

____ bayou lout   C. Kidnapped New Orleans' boy

____ cat's cradle   D. Slaving ship

____ pressed   E. Corner of St. Louis and Chartres Streets

____ Bollweevil   F. Purvis and Mary played this with Jessie

____ Purvis   G. Slave trade

____ thirteen   H. Captain's nickname for Jessie

____ chloride of lime   I. Aunt Agatha's name for Jessie

____ shrouds   J. Jessie did this under an apothecary

____ Jessie   K. Slave dancer's age

____ The Moonlight   L. Pressganged or forced into ship's service

____ Black Gold   M. Ropes that support the mast

____ apprentice   N. Kidnapper Jessie came to trust

____ British Blockade   O. Old black Mississippian man

The Slave Dancer Advanced Short Answer Unit Test Page 2

II. Short Answer

1. Explain the significance of the ship's name, *The Moonlight*.

2. How did the slaves in the hold treat Jessie when Stout lowered him down into the hold to retrieve his fife? Why do you think they behaved in this manner?

3. What does the New Orleans' slave woman "Star" represent to Jessie?

4. Explain what Purvis was referring to when he told Jessie they'd have a ship full of *royalty* for him to play for.

5. Reveal the contradiction within Wick's statement to Cooley," Leave off with your birds! It's only savages who'd take pleasure in such a spectacle."

6. Why do you think the author based the story on a *shipwrecked* slave ship? What does the shipwreck symbolize?

The Slave Dancer Advanced Short Answer Unit Test Page 3

7. Explain Jessie's statement upon returning to New Orleans, "I made a promise to myself: I would do nothing that was connected ever so faintly with the importing and sale and use of slaves. But I soon discovered that everything I considered bore, somewhere along the way, the imprint of black hands."

III. Essay

Purvis reacted violently to Jessie's criticism of the whole business of slaving. Using evidence from the text, explain **his** justification in your own words. Do you feel it is an understandable or reasonable one? Why or why not?

The Slave Dancer Advanced Short Answer Unit Test Page 4

IV. Vocabulary

Listen to the vocabulary words and write them down. After you have written down all the words, write a paragraph in which you use all the words. The paragraph must in some way relate to *The Slave Dancer*.

MULTIPLE CHOICE UNIT TEST 1 - *The Slave Dancer*

I. Matching

1. Bollweevil
2. The Moonlight
3. chloride of lime
4. thirteen
5. pressed
6. Daniel
7. cat's cradle
8. slave market
9. bayou lout
10. British Blockade
11. Black Gold
12. Purvis
13. Jessie
14. apprentice
15. shrouds

A. Englishmen trying to stop slave trade
B. Used to try to clear stench from the holds
C. Kidnapped New Orleans' boy
D. Slaving ship
E. Corner of St. Louis and Chartres Streets
F. Purvis and Mary played this with Jessie
G. Slave trade
H. Captain's nickname for Jessie
I. Aunt Agatha's name for Jessie
J. Jessie did this under an apothecary
K. Slave dancer's age
L. Pressganged or forced into ship's service
M. Ropes that support the mast
N. Kidnapper Jessie came to trust
O. Old black Mississippian man

The Slave Dancer Multiple Choice Unit Test 1 page 2

II. Multiple Choice

1. On his way home from Aunt Agatha's, Jessie
   a. trips on his fife
   b. runs away
   c. sees Star, a slave woman
   d. is kidnapped

2. Jessie finds himself
   a. at the slave market
   b. on a raft
   c. in the sea
   d. on a sailing ship

3. Jessie was needed by these men to
   a. play his instrument
   b. play with the young slave children
   c. catch rats
   d. all of the above

4. Slave trading was hazardous because
   a. the Quakers would prosecute
   b. Spanish flags were illegal
   c. British and U.S. groups could stop them
   d. Blackbeard was looking for them

5. When the ship had becalmed
   a. gratings replaced the hatches
   b. tempers flared
   c. a huge cauldron appeared in the galley
   d. all of the above

6. One of the crew members was flogged because
   a. an egg was stolen from the Captain
   b. the Captain needed to remind the men
   c. Purvis hurt Ben Stout
   d. both a and b

The Slave Dancer Multiple Choice Unit Test 1 page 3

7. Slaving ships used different flags
    a. for different routes
    b. to try to avoid arrest and penalty
    c. warn the Revenue Cutters
    d. save wear and tear on their main flag

8. Upon seeing land, Jessie
    a. jumps off the ship.
    b. goes into a dark mood
    c. seeks an escape plan
    d. hides on the tween deck

9. When Jessie criticized slaving
    a. Purvis became defensive
    b. the Captain slapped him
    c. Stout flogged him
    d. Cooley threw his flute into the holds

10. *The Moonlight* left Whydah
    a. at night
    b. after the Spaniard inspected the load
    c. at dawn
    d. in the late afternoon

11. Which crew member admitted to the evils of slaving?
    a. Stout
    b. Cawthorne
    c. Ned

12. Jessie defies orders to play for the slaves because
    a. Stout made him go down into the holds
    b. he can't stand it one more minute
    c. he is mad at the Captain
    d. Purvis addles him

The Slave Dancer Multiple Choice Unit Test 1 page 4

13. Jessie is able to escape temporarily from the horrors of the ship by
    a. playing his flute for the men
    b. hiding in his hammock
    c. recalling details of his homeplace
    d. all of the above

14. Purvis characterized Stout as
    a. a dead man
    b. a traitor to the crew
    c. a bitter old man
    d. a puppet on a string

15. If he makes it home, Jessie vows never again to visit
    a. the wharf
    b. Aunt Agatha's
    c. the Slave Market
    d. Congo Square

16. Stored in the chest Jessie retrieved from the Captain were
    a. biscuits
    b. clothes
    c. used leg chains
    d. rum bottles

17. The Captain ordered the slaves overboard when
    a. the mutiny began
    b. Stout said to
    c. the Spaniard rejected them
    d. an American ship approached

18. Find what Jessie says while swimming to shore.
    a. Hold on Ras!
    b. Oh! Swim!
    c. Don't let it get you down!

19. Ras eventually went
    a. back to live with Daniel
    b. to the North
    c. back to Wydah

The Slave Dancer Multiple Choice Unit Test 1 page 5

20. The most long-lasting effect on Jessie from his ordeal was
    a. his mother's fear
    b. his repulsion to music
    c. the scar on his back
    d. his memory of Purvis

III. Quotations: Identify the speaker:

A= Aunt Agatha   B= Jessie   C= Captain   D= Clay Purvis
E= Ned Grime   F= Ben Stout   G= Ras   H= Mrs. Bollier

1. "What an undignified way to earn your keep! Playing that silly pipe! It's time you were apprenticed and learned a trade. I doubt you'd benefit from schooling."

2. "Take up that pipe, Claudius. He's worth nothing without his pipe."

3. "No, no. Not playing for the Captain, but for kings and princes and other such like trash. Why, we'll have a ship full of royalty, won't we?"

4. "They've different laws than us. They've entirely stopped the slave trade in their own country- the worse for them- and would like us to copy them in their folly. Why, the trade is the best trade there is our trade goods, they sell their people cheaper that they ever did to tempt us to run the British blockade. So we profit despite the damned Englishmen."

5. "Yes. I'm a tight packer, as neat as a pin, stack them up like flannel cakes, one on top of the other. Ah- it's the British who've forced me to be so ingenious."

6. "The African was tempted and then became depraved by a desire for the material things offered him by debased traders. It's all the Devil's work."

7. "You're not so young you don't know what an order is."

8. "I have a touch of death. Haven't you heard of the wages of sin? Did you think they were gold?"

9. "I can't hear it! I can't bear it!"

10. "Yes. That's what I think. Someone has taken it and dropped it down to the niggers so's they can play their own tunes."

11. "Jessie? Nose. Teef. Jessie."

12. I made a promise to myself: I would do nothing that was connected ever so faintly with the importing and sale and use of slaves. But I soon discovered that everything I considered bore, somewhere along the way, the imprint of black hands."

The Slave Dancer Multiple Choice Unit Test 1 page 6
IV. Vocabulary (Matching)

1. barbarousness   A. foul
2. armament   B. arms; weapons
3. confounding   C. dense; thick
4. demented   D. horribly cruel
5. envisage   E. dangerous
6. fetid   F. pictured
7. impenetrable   G. puzzling; flustering
8. impertinent   H. glowing; radiant
9. jettison   I. shamed; embarrassed
10. languorous   J. crazy; mad
11. lucrative   K. unknown; unfamiliar
12. luminous   L. excess
13. mortified   M. control; restriction
14. obscure   N. profitable
15. perilous   O. sassy; fresh
16. profusion   P. tied up
17. restraint   Q. sleepy; lazy
18. shambling   R. abandon; get rid of
19. trussed   S. unstopped
20. undeterred   T. shuffling

Multiple Choice Unit Test 2 - *The Slave Dancer*

I. Matching

1. Daniel
2. slave market
3. bayou lout
4. cat's cradle
5. pressed
6. Bollweevil
7. Purvis
8. thirteen
9. chloride of lime
10. shrouds
11. Jessie
12. The Moonlight
13. Black Gold
14. apprentice
15. British Blockade

A. Englishmen trying to stop slave trade
B. Used to try to clear stench from the holds
C. Kidnapped New Orleans' boy
D. Slaving ship
E. Corner of St. Louis and Chartres Streets
F. Purvis and Mary played this with Jessie
G. Slave trade
H. Captain's nickname for Jessie
I. Aunt Agatha's name for Jessie
J. Jessie did this under an apothecary
K. Slave dancer's age
L. Pressganged or forced into ship's service
M. Ropes that support the mast
N. Kidnapper Jessie came to trust
O. Old black Mississippian man

The Slave Dancer Multiple Choice Unit Test 2 page 2

II. Multiple Choice

1. Jessie's mother is a
    a. seamtress
    b. waitress
    c. servant
    d. nurse

2. Jessie's father
    a. deserted his family
    b. drowned in the Mississippi
    c. fell off a steamboat
    d. lived in Massachusetts

3. Near the rich families' walls, Jessie is reminded of
    a. his errand
    b. the slave, 'Star'
    c. his lateness
    d. his poorness

4. One of Jessie's kidnappers
    a. paid him two pennies
    b. ate oranges at the dock
    c. had him play a martial tune
    d. all of the above

5. The Captain will give what in exchange for the slaves?
    a. rum
    b. money
    c. tobacco
    d. all of the above

6. The British try to blockade other slave traders because
    a. they want the profits for themselves
    b. they want to add ships totheir fleet
    c. the queen ordered it
    d. they have stopped doing it and want others also to stop

The Slave Dancer Multiple Choice Unit Test 2 page 3

7. Choose the one job Jessie did not do on the ship during the day.
    a. track the rats
    b. mend sails
    c. cook meals
    d. heave waste over the side

8. When the ship had becalmed
    a. gratings replaced the hatches
    b. tempers flared
    c. a huge cauldron appeared in the galley
    d. all of the above

9. Who was wrongfully accused and flogged for stealing the egg?
    a. Purvis
    b. Stout
    c. Jessie
    d. Ned

10. Slaving ships used different flags
    a. for different routes
    b. to try to avoid arrest and penalty
    c. warn the Revenue Cutters
    d. save wear and tear on their main flag

11. Jessie must play his fife to
    a. exercise the crew
    b. dance the slaves
    c. satisfy the Captain
    d. practice for Mardi Gras

12. Upon seeing land, Jessie
    a. jumps off the ship.
    b. falls into a dark mood
    c. seeks an escape plan
    d. hides on the tween deck

The Slave Dancer Multiple Choice Unit Test 2 page 4

13. When Jessie criticized slaving
    a. Purvis became defensive
    b. the Captain slapped him
    c. Stout flogged him
    d. Cooley threw his flute into the holds

14. Ned smacked Jessie because
    a. he cried out
    b. he didn't do his job
    c. he smiled at the slaves
    d. he refused to play

15. If the slaves will not dance they
    a. are whipped or stepped on
    b. get sent to the holds
    c. don't receive dinner
    d. have to play the flute

16. Jessie defies orders to play for the slaves because
    a. Stout made him go down into the holds
    b. he can't stand it one more minute
    c. he is mad at the Captain
    d. Purvis addles him

17. Jessie is able to escape temporarily from the horrors of the ship by
    a. playing his flute for the men
    b. hiding in his hammock
    c. recalling details of his homeplace
    d. all of the above

18. The Captain ordered the slaves overboard when
    a. the mutiny began
    b. Stout said to
    c. the Spaniard rejected them
    d. an American ship approached

The Slave Dancer Multiple Choice Unit Test 2 page 5

19. Find what Jessie says while swimming to shore.
    a. Hold on Ras!
    b. Oh! Swim!
    c. Don't let it get you down!
    d. This is how my father drowned.

20. Jessie's mother
    a. questioned the market venders daily for news of Jessie
    b. thought him dead
    c. couldn't bear the fate of the slaves
    d. all of the above

The Slave Dancer Multiple Choice Unit Test 2 page 6

III. Quotations: Identify the speaker:

A= Captain   B= Clay Purvis   C= Ben Stout   D= Ned Grime
E=Mrs. Bollier   F= Jessie   G= Aunt Agatha   H= Ras

1. "What an undignified way to earn your keep! Playing that silly pipe! It's time you were apprenticed and learned a trade. I doubt you'd benefit from schooling."

2. "Take up that pipe, Claudius. He's worth nothing without his pipe."

3. "No, no. Not playing for the Captain, but for kings and princes and other such like trash. Why, we'll have a ship full of royalty, won't we?"

4. "They've different laws than us. They've entirely stopped the slave trade in their own country- the worse for them- and would like us to copy them in their folly. Why, the trade is the best trade there is our trade goods, they sell their people cheaper that they ever did to tempt us to run the British blockade. So we profit despite the damned Englishmen."

5. "Yes. I'm a tight packer, as neat as a pin, stack them up like flannel cakes, one on top of the other. Ah- it's the British who've forced me to be so ingenious."

6. "The African was tempted and then became depraved by a desire for the material things offered him by debased traders. It's all the Devil's work."

7. "You're not so young you don't know what an order is."

8. "I have a touch of death. Haven't you heard of the wages of sin? Did you think they were gold?"

9. "I Can't hear it! I can't bear it!"

10. "Yes. That's what I think. Someone has taken it and dropped it down to the niggers so's they can play their own tunes."

11. "Jessie? Nose. Teef. Jessie."

12. "I made a promise to myself: I would do nothing that was connected ever so faintly with the importing and sale and use of slaves. But I soon discovered that everything I considered bore, somewhere along the way, the imprint of black hands."

The Slave Dancer Multiple Choice Unit Test 2 page 7

IV. Vocabulary (Matching)

1. barbarousness
2. lucrative
3. confounding
4. jettison
5. envisaged
6. impertinent
7. impenetrable
8. armament
9. fetid
10. mortified
11. demented
12. undeterred
13. languorous
14. restrain
15. trussed
16. profusion
17. obscure
18. shambling
19. perilous
20. luminous

A. foul
B. arms; weapons
C. dense; thick
D. horribly cruel
E. dangerous
F. pictured
G. puzzling; flustering
H. glowing; radiant
I. shamed; embarrassed
J. crazy; mad
K. unknown; unfamiliar
L. excess
M. control; restriction
N. profitable
O. sassy; fresh
P. tied up
Q. sleepy; lazy
R. abandon; get rid of
S. unstopped
T. shuffling

ANSWER SHEET: MULTIPLE CHOICE UNIT TESTS - *The Slave Dancer*

I. Matching

1. ___
2. ___
3. ___
4. ___
5. ___
6. ___
7. ___
8. ___
9. ___
10. ___
11. ___
12. ___
13. ___
14. ___
15. ___

II. Multiple Choice

1. (A) (B) (C) (D)
2. (A) (B) (C) (D)
3. (A) (B) (C) (D)
4. (A) (B) (C) (D)
5. (A) (B) (C) (D)
6. (A) (B) (C) (D)
7. (A) (B) (C) (D)
8. (A) (B) (C) (D)
9. (A) (B) (C) (D)
10. (A) (B) (C) (D)
11. (A) (B) (C) (D)
12. (A) (B) (C) (D)
13. (A) (B) (C) (D)
14. (A) (B) (C) (D)
15. (A) (B) (C) (D)
16. (A) (B) (C) (D)
17. (A) (B) (C) (D)
18. (A) (B) (C) (D)
19. (A) (B) (C) (D)
20. (A) (B) (C) (D)

III. Quotes

1. (A) (B) (C) (D) (E) (F) (G) (H)
2. (A) (B) (C) (D) (E) (F) (G) (H)
3. (A) (B) (C) (D) (E) (F) (G) (H)
4. (A) (B) (C) (D) (E) (F) (G) (H)
5. (A) (B) (C) (D) (E) (F) (G) (H)
6. (A) (B) (C) (D) (E) (F) (G) (H)
7. (A) (B) (C) (D) (E) (F) (G) (H)
8. (A) (B) (C) (D) (E) (F) (G) (H)
9. (A) (B) (C) (D) (E) (F) (G) (H)
10. (A) (B) (C) (D) (E) (F) (G) (H)
11. (A) (B) (C) (D) (E) (F) (G) (H)
12. (A) (B) (C) (D) (E) (F) (G) (H)

IV. Vocabulary

1. ___
2. ___
3. ___
4. ___
5. ___
6. ___
7. ___
8. ___
9. ___
10. ___
11. ___
12. ___
13. ___
14. ___
15. ___
16. ___
17. ___
18. ___
19. ___
20. ___

ANSWER SHEET KEY - *The Slave Dancer*
Multiple Choice Unit Test 1

I. Matching
1. H
2. D
3. B
4. K
5. L
6. O
7. F
8. E
9. I
10. A
11. G
12. N
13. C
14. J
15. N

II. Multiple Choice
1. (A) (B) (C) ( )
2. (A) ( ) (C) (D)
3. ( ) (B) (C) (D)
4. (A) (B) ( ) (D)
5. (A) (B) (C) ( )
6. (A) (B) (C) ( )
7. (A) ( ) (C) ( )
8. (A) ( ) (C) (D)
9. ( ) (B) (C) (D)
10. ( ) (B) (C) (D)
11. (A) (B) ( ) (D)
12. (A) ( ) (C) (D)
13. (A) (B) ( ) (D)
14. ( ) (B) (C) (D)
15. (A) (B) ( ) (D)
16. (A) ( ) (C) (D)
17. (A) (B) (C) ( )
18. (A) ( ) (C) (D)
19. (A) ( ) (C) (D)
20. (A) ( ) (C) (D)

III. Quotes
1. (A) (B) (C) (D) (E) (F) ( ) (H)
2. (A) ( ) (C) (D) (E) (F) (G) (H)
3. (A) ( ) (C) (D) (E) (F) (G) (H)
4. (A) ( ) (C) (D) (E) (F) (G) (H)
5. ( ) (B) (C) (D) (E) (F) (G) (H)
6. (A) (B) (C) ( ) (E) (F) (G) (H)
7. ( ) (B) (C) (D) (E) (F) (G) (H)
8. (A) (B) (C) ( ) (E) (F) (G) (H)
9. (A) (B) (C) (D) ( ) (F) (G) (H)
10. (A) (B) ( ) (D) (E) (F) (G) (H)
11. (A) (B) (C) (D) (E) (F) (G) ( )
12. (A) (B) (C) (D) (E) ( ) (G) (H)

IV. Vocabulary
1. D
2. B
3. G
4. J
5. F
6. A
7. C
8. O
9. R
10. Q
11. N
12. H
13. I
14. K
15. E
16. L
17. N
18. T
19. P
20. S

ANSWER SHEET KEY - *The Slave Dancer*
Multiple Choice Unit Test 2

I. Matching
1. L
2. E
3. I
4. F
5. L
6. H
7. N
8. K
9. B
10. M
11. C
12. D
13. G
14. J
15. A

II. Multiple Choice
1. ( ) (B) (C) (D)
2. (A) ( ) (C) (D)
3. (A) ( ) (C) (D)
7. (A) (B) ( ) (D)
8. (A) (B) (C) ( )
9. ( ) (B) (C) (D)
10. (A) ( ) (C) (D)
11. (A) ( ) (C) (D)
12. (A) ( ) (C) (D)
13. ( ) (B) (C) (D)
14. ( ) (B) (C) (D)
15. ( ) (B) (C) (D)
16. (A) ( ) (C) (D)
17. (A) (B) ( ) (D)
18. (A) (B) (C) ( )
19. (A) ( ) (C) (D)
20. (A) (B) (C) ( )

III. Quotes
1. (A) (B) (C) (D) (E) (F) ( ) (H)
2. (A) (B) (C) (D) ( ) (F) (G) (H)
3. (A) (B) (C) ( ) (E) (F) (G) (H)
4. (A) (B) (C) (D) (E) (F) (G) ( )
5. ( ) (B) (C) (D) (E) (F) (G) (H)
6. (A) (B) (C) (D) (E) ( ) (G) (H)
7. (A) (B) (C) (D) (E) ( ) (G) (H)
8. (A) ( ) (C) (D) (E) (F) (G) (H)
9. (A) (B) (C) (D) (E) (F) ( ) (H)
10. (A) (B) (C) (D) (E) (F) (G) ( )
11. (A) (B) ( ) (D) (E) (F) (G) (H)
12. (A) (B) ( ) (D) (E) (F) (G) (H)

IV. Vocabulary
1. D
2. N
3. G
4. R
5. F
6. O
7. C
8. B
9. A
10. I
11. J
12. S
13. Q
14. M
15. P
16. L
17. K
18. T
19. E
20. H

UNIT RESOURCE MATERIALS

BULLETIN BOARD IDEAS - *The Slave Dancer*

1. Save a space for students' best writing. Make a border or graphic that illustrates the topic of their writing. Musical notes or flutes would do for the writing on the role music plays in their lives. Staple up the best writing samples (or quizzes or whatever you have graded) on colorful paper.

2. Bring in (or have students bring in) pictures of slaving ships, Cuba, New Orleans, Nigeria, etc. Make a collage if you have enough different pictures (or post individual pictures on colorful paper if you only have a few pictures). This could also be a fun introductory activity for students to create a quick bulletin board.

3. Draw one of the word search puzzles onto the bulletin board. (Be sure to enlarge it.) Write the key words to one side. Invite students to take their pens or markers and find the words before and/or after class (or perhaps this could be an activity for students who finish their work early).

4. Have artistic students create a mural depicting the route taken on this voyage, labeling it accurately.

5. Students could write pretend diaries, illustrating them with sketches. These could be for any of the slaves, crew, or Jessie's mother or sister. Display when completed.

6. Students could do a study of the constellation appropriate to *The Moonlight's* route, and then post with information on how sailors used it to guide their ships..

7. Graphically compare Jessie's life in New Orleans with his existence on the ship, or have your students compare their lifestyles with Jessie's.

8. Create a detailed illustration of *The Moonlight*.

9. Musical students could compose and perform a selection typical of what they think Jessie played for the slaves. Keep the word *martial* in mind. The music could be posted and illustrated.

10. Create a composite of the crew members, surrounding them with elements and details that illustrate each of them personally.

11. Design an illustrated representation of Jessie's journey from Daniel's in Mississippi to his home in the French Quarter.

12. Depict Ras's journey north with the two black men. Decide where you think his destination was and include it.

Bulletin Board Ideas *Slave Dancer* Continued

13. Post illustrations of figurative language from the book.

14. Recreate the barren island Jessie saw as the ship neared Cuban waters and the colorful flying fish they saw jumping out of the water near it.

15. Have students design a mural which shows a slave market scene.

16. Draw a large map showing the Triangle Trade route from North America to Africa to the West Indies. Explain (using symbols and a map legend) each location's profit and contribution to the slave trading.

EXTRA ACTIVITIES - *The Slave Dancer*

One of the difficulties in teaching a novel is that all students don't read at the same speed. One student who likes to read may take the book home and finish it in a day or two. Sometimes a few students finish the in-class assignments early. The problem, then, is finding suitable extra activities for students.

One thing you can do is keep a little library in the classroom. For this unit on *The Slave Dancer*, you might check out from the school library other books by Paula Fox. A biography of the author would be interesting for some students. You may include other related books and articles about: slavery, the Middle Passage, abolitionists, slave uprisings, slave markets, Nigerian African tribes and their cultures, pressganging, the Underground Railroad, the Emancipation Proclamation, Cuban sugar plantations, etc.

Other things you may keep on hand are puzzles. We have made some relating directly to *The Slave Dancer* for you. Feel free to duplicate them.

Some students may like to draw. You might devise a contest or allow some extra-credit grade for students who draw scenes from *The Slave Dancer* such as: the fire in the barracoon, the storm and shipwreck, Jessie dancing the slaves, Jessie in the holds, Stout stealing the egg, etc. Note, too, that if the students do not want to keep their drawings you may pick up some extra bulletin board materials this way. If you have a contest and you supply the prize or, you could possibly make the drawing itself a non-refundable entry fee.

The pages which follow contain games, puzzles and worksheets. The keys, when appropriate, immediately follow the puzzle or worksheet. There are two main groups of activities: one group for the unit; that is, generally relating to *The Slave Dancer* text, and another group of activities related strictly to *The Slave Dancer* vocabulary.

Directions for the games, puzzles and worksheets are self-explanatory. The object here is to provide you with extra materials you may use in any way you choose.

MORE ACTIVITIES - *The Slave Dancer*

1. Pick a chapter or scene with a great deal of dialogue and have the students act it out on a stage. (Perhaps you could assign various scenes to different groups of students so more than one scene could be acted and more students could participate

2. Write an account of Daniel's escape and relocation to the Mississippi shore.

3. Create a Cereal Box Book for *The Slave Dancer*. Students take an empty cereal box, cover it with construction paper and turn it into what looks like a large book. *Front panel*: title, illustration, author, and short summary. *First side*: List of characters *Second side or spine*: Name of book (*The Slave Dancer*) *Back panel*: Game or contest pertaining to book These look nice lined up next to each other like a real shelf of books. (Encourage a variety of paper colors, inks, markers, etc.)

4. Promote model builders to try to recreate *The Moonlight*.

5. Research maritime injustice in the 1800's. Have a group report findings to the class. See if they can relate what they found to what happened on *The Moonlight*.

6. Use some of the related topics (noted earlier for an in-class library) as topics for other research, reports or written papers, or as topics for guest speakers.

7. Have students plan and teach a lesson on a chapter or section of the book. Give them guidelines and a time-frame.

8. Have a Cat's Cradle string game tournament.

9. Invite a speaker to share on fabrics used by Jessie's mother. Perhaps a home economics teacher could enlighten the class on the difficulty of this profession in the 1800's as compared to modern times and show fabric samples. Taking the idea even further, girls could dress up in gowns fashioned from these fabrics of the period, if some could be located and borrowed.

10. Write to Paula Fox asking her questions students have composed. You could send a class set of letters in one large envelope.

11. Write a diary entry for one of grown-up Jessie's days in Andersonville at the end of the Civil War. Relate to his experience on the ship.

12. Have a group of students research available film connections to this unit. Show some of their choices. Compare to the book. (Alex Haley's *Roots* is one example.)

More Activities - *The Slave Dancer* Page 2

13. Study the climate of New Orleans comparing it to that of where Jessie and his family relocate, Rhode Island, or to where your students live.

14. Research diseases mentioned in the book and chart the death rate on the ship from each, based on information in the book.

15. Read one or more accounts of famous black Americans noting their achievements. Also review accounts of slave escapes and uprisings. (Frederick Douglas, Gabriel Prosser, Nat Turner, Denmark Vesey, Crispus Attucks, Tituba, etc.) Have a group report their findings.

16. Allow students to select a character from the novel. Have them dress like them, speak like them; assume their persona. Create a talk show format with these characters as the guests. Have a student volunteer to be the host. Others not involved will be the audience; questioning the characters. Have a topic like: cruelty, discrimination, power, fear, or greed- themes encountered in the novel. Allow the class to decide as much as possible. Have questions from the audience ready prior to the show day. You could have students try out for the parts. Remind them to keep it on the up and up, not to mimic some of the seedier talk shows. This will require students to take an in-depth look into the characterization in the novel.

17. Students who like board games may want to create one using information from this novel. Some students could work together as a group to complete this task. Encourage them to look at setting to illustrate their board and possibly use vocabulary, characters, plot, etc. for question cards.

18. Read selections from *The Dark -Thirty, Southern Tales of the Supernatural* aloud to the class. The first one, "The Legend of Pin Oak " is especially appropriate. Two other noteworthy books to read parts of are *Mississippi Challenge* by Mildred Pitts Walter and *Freedom's Children*.

19. Hold a debate on the issue of slavery.

20. Make up stories of lost ships like the ones the crew told Jessie. Have a story-telling session.

21. Research Harriet Tubman and the Underground Railroad. Write and act out a play depicting one of her journeys North.

22. Write dialogue and act it out for a chance meeting between Ras and Jessie in New England after the Civil War ended and Jessie returned home.

23. Find out about the "flying fish" Purvis and Jessie saw spring from the sea. Recreate the impression of the one on his mother's sewing box.

WORD SEARCH - *The Slave Dancer*

All words in this list are associated with *The Slave Dancer*. The words are placed backwards, forward, diagonally, up and down. The clues below the word search can help you find the words.

```
B E N I N E K C I H C T H I R T E E N C A S K S
V E X G L X L L T B D U B C K L L Q O M U R A R
K I T D S G M O T T L O R M A D K N M W A B K R
D T E T E N R F E R S O K R A O G L G P M S A S
F E W U Y S S R S R E Q C R Y O R R S H A R K S
N C B K X R S D K C C S C K Y B R K P M C J L F
C G N B E L U E I J A G W R A S E C C H R T D K
V X M T V O Y T R N Q W P H R D B A A O M L W V
T L T N R M N M D P V J T E R X E R U N C M X X
P U G H X E S L A A D T E H K C L F A L D K H V
C P S N R F N L M C N T K S O E A G F G I L M H
M J B P K R L B A F A I W X S R S F A Y A E E Z
R F P O B L A Y Q V L R E T D I N I R L M T U S
H A M M O C K I F E B O L L W E E V I L S H N
Z F T U K M W R T N B N O O F I P C W R C E K A
M K T S G H P L J H G G S Y N O M S Y Q U A Y Q
M O O N L I G H T E K C U B H B B E N E D P X B
```

AFRICA	CAWTHORNE	GALLEY	PRIVATEERS
AGATHA	CHARLESTON	GOLD	PURVIS
APPRENTICE	CHICKEN	HAMMOCK	RAFT
BEAULIEU	COCKROACH	HOPE	RAS
BEN	CONGO	IBOS	SHARKS
BENIN	CRADLE	JESSIE	SHROUDS
BETTY	CREOLE	LIME	SLAVE
BLOCKADE	CUBA	LOUT	SPARK
BOLLWEEVIL	CURRY	MACAROON	STAR
BOOM	CUTTERS	MOONLIGHT	SWIM
BUCKET	DANIEL	NED	THIRTEEN
CANDLES	FIFE	NEEDLE	VIEUX
CASKS	FLYING	PRESSED	

CROSSWORD - *The Slave Dancer*

CROSSWORD CLUES - *The Slave Dancer*

ACROSS

1. Kidnapped New Orleans boy; ___ Bollier
7. Captain's nickname for Jessie
9. Cat's ___; Purvis & Mary played this with Jessie
11. Irish ___; Captain's nickname for Purvis
12. Old black man in Mississippi
13. Slave woman Jessie saw in the Vieux Carre
16. The ___; slaving ship
19. Object used to support Bollier family
20. Slave Dancer's age
22. Black boy who survives with Jessie
23. African bay; Bight of ___
25. Place where slaves will be sold
27. Also
28. Crescent-mouthed maggots with stitched teeth
31. Patrols U.S. shores; U.S. Revenue ___
33. Coordinating conjunction
34. Ras and Jessie hung onto it while trying to reach shore
35. Man's title
36. Wooden kegs in hold that held water
39. Jessie's instrument
40. A single; uno
41. Jessie did this under an apothecary
42. Slang for 'father'
43. First Mate

DOWN

2. ___ Market; located on corner of St. Louis and Chartres Streets
3. Oh, ___! Jessie's plea of hope
4. Christian ship carpenter
5. ___ Carre; New Orleans French Quarter
6. Black ___; nickname for slave trade
7. ___ Stout; took Spark's place
8. Bayou ___; Aunt Agatha's name for Jessie
9. ___ Square; New Orleans spot for slave festivities
10. Jessie's father's French surname
14. Aunt ___; Jessie's dead father's cranky sister
15. Jessie's sister
16. Defective black
17. Used to try to clear stench from the hold; chloride of ___
18. Opposite of bottom
21. Captain won't take any
23. Englishmen trying to stop slave trade
24. The one after this one
25. Ship's cook
26. Pressganged or forced into ship's service
29. Jessie's bed on the ship
30. Ropes that support the mast
32. Pushed Jessie on while dogpawing
37. Pass over
38. Opposite of down

CROSSWORD ANSWER KEY - *The Slave Dancer*

MATCHING QUIZ/WORKSHEET 1 - *The Slave Dancer*

___ 1. U. S. Revenue Cutters   A. Defective black

___ 2. Bight of Benin   B. Needed by Jessie's mother to sew at night

___ 3. Vieux Carre   C. New Orleans' French Quarter

___ 4. Charleston   D. Louisianian of French ancestry

___ 5. Ben Stout   E. Jessie's instrument

___ 6. Ned Grime   F. Patrols U. S. shores

___ 7. Macaroon   G. Ship's kitchen

___ 8. Candles   H. Object used to support the Bollier family

___ 9. Needle   I. African bay

___ 10. Ras   J. Final destination of *The Moonlight*

___ 11. Boom   K. Ship's Christian carpenter

___ 12. Daniel   L. Took Spark's place

___ 13. Star   M. Old Mississippi black man

___ 14. Fox   N. Wooden kegs kept in the hold that held water

___ 15. Casks   O. The boys hung unto it until they reached shore

___ 16. Cuba   P. Jessie's sister

___ 17. Betty   Q. Slave woman Jessie saw in the French Quarter

___ 18. Galley   R. Place where slaves are to be sold

___ 19. Creole   S. Author

___ 20. Fife   T. Black boy who survived with Jessie

KEY: MATCHING QUIZ/WORKSHEET 1 - *The Slave Dancer*

F	1. U. S. Revenue Cutters	A.	Defective black
I	2. Bight of Benin	B.	Needed by Jessie's mother to sew at night
C	3. Vieux Carre	C.	New Orleans' French Quarter
J	4. Charleston	D.	Louisianian of French ancestry
L	5. Ben Stout	E.	Jessie's instrument
K	6. Ned Grime	F.	Patrols U. S. shores
A	7. Macaroon	G.	Ship's kitchen
B	8. Candles	H.	Object used to support the Bollier family
H	9. Needle	I.	African bay
T	10. Ras	J.	Final destination of *The Moonlight*
O	11. Boom	K.	Ship's Christian carpenter
M	12. Daniel	L.	Took Spark's place
Q	13. Star	M.	Old Mississippi black man
S	14. Fox	N.	Wooden kegs kept in the hold that held water
N	15. Casks	O.	The boys hung unto it until they reached shore
R	16. Cuba	P.	Jessie's sister
P	17. Betty	Q.	Slave woman Jessie saw in the French Quarter
G	18. Galley	R.	Place where slaves are to be sold
D	19. Creole	S.	Author
E	20. Fife	T.	Black boy who survived with Jessie

MATCHING QUIZ/WORKSHEET 2 - *The Slave Dancer*

___ 1. Congo Square   A. Carved on Jessie's mother's sewing box

___ 2. Agatha   B. Individuals profiting on slave trade

___ 3. Flying fish   C. Jessie's bed on the ship

___ 4. Privateers   D. Oddly comforting sight to Jessie upon waking

___ 5. Irish Bucket   E. New Orleans's spot for slave festivity

___ 6. Ben Stout   F. Ship's cook

___ 7. Cawthorne   G. Crescent-mouthed maggots with stitched teeth

___ 8. Cockroach   H. First mate on the ship

___ 9. Beaulieu   I. Jessie's aunt

___10. Oh! Swim!   J. Captain won't take any

___12. Chicken   L. Captain of *The Moonlight*

___13. Sharks   M. Captain's nickname for Purvis

___14. Hammock   N. Jessie's father's French surname

___15. Curry   O. Where slaves will be picked up

___16. Spark   P. Claudius and Purvis dumped Jessie on this

___17. Ibos   Q. Took Spark's place

___18. Hope   R. Jessie's plea of hope

___19. Raft   S Pushed Jessie on while dogpawing

___20. Africa   T. First sign of life on deserted shore

158

KEY: MATCHING QUIZ/WORKSHEET 2 - *The Slave Dancer*

_E_	1. Congo Square	A. Carved on Jessie's mother's sewing box
_I_	2. Agatha	B. Individuals profiting on slave trade
_A_	3. Flying fish	C. Jessie's bed on the ship
_B_	4. Privateers	D. Oddly comforting sight to Jessie upon waking
_M_	5. Irish Bucket	E. New Orleans's spot for slave festivity
_Q_	6. Ben Stout	F. Ship's cook
_L_	7. Cawthorne	G. Crescent-mouthed maggots with stitched teeth
_D_	8. Cockroach	H. First mate on the ship
_N_	9. Beaulieu	I. Jessie's aunt
_R_	10. Oh! Swim!	J. Captain won't take any
_T_	12. Chicken	L. Captain of *The Moonlight*
_G_	13. Sharks	M. Captain's nickname for Purvis
_C_	14. Hammock	N. Jessie's father's French surname
_F_	15. Curry	O. Where slaves will be picked up
_H_	16. Spark	P. Claudius and Purvis dumped Jessie on this
_J_	17. Ibos	Q. Took Spark's place
_S_	18. Hope	R. Jessie's plea of hope
_P_	19. Raft	S Pushed Jessie on while dogpawing
_O_	20. Africa	T. First sign of life on deserted shore

JUGGLE LETTER REVIEW GAME CLUE SHEET - *The Slave Dancer*

SCRAMBLED	WORD	CLUE
FOIHGNETINBB	BIGHT OF BENIN	African Bay
GOTEHHTONMLI	THE MOONLIGHT	Slaving ship
SHOWMI	OH SWIM!	Jessie's plea of hope
LLAOKBCDG	BLACK GOLD	Slave trade
UUEEBAIL	BEAULIEU	Jessie's father's French surname
CHOMKMA	HAMMOCK	Jessie's bed on ship
ASR	RAS	Black boy who survives with Jessie
PHOE	HOPE	Pushed Jessie on while dogpawing
RYRUC	CURRY	Ship's cook
EELORC	CREOLE	Louisianian of French ancestory
LEADIN	DANIEL	Old black man in Mississippi
EFIF	FIFE	Jessie's instrument
QSOOCNGRUERA	CONGO SQUARE	New Orleans' spot for slave festivity
ELCCTAADRC	CAT'S CRADLE	Purvis and Mary played this with Jess
XEUCRVIEAR	VIEUX CARRE	New Orlean's French Quarter
ELVOBWLLIL	BOLLWEEVIL	Captain's nickname for Jessie
ERRPIAVEST	PRIVATEERS	Individuals profiting on slave trade
TRAPEERICN	APPRENTICE	Jessie did this under an apothecary
UNTTBESO	BEN STOUT	Took Spark's place
WEACHTNOR	CAWTHORNE	Captain of *The Moonlight*
MEDINGRE	NED GRIME	Christian ship carpenter
HRCCOOKCA	COCKROACH	Oddly comforting to Jessie
DRUOHSS	SHROUDS	Ropes that support the mast
DELEEN	NEEDLE	Object that supports Bollier family
VPRSIU	PURVIS	Kidnapper turned friend
LEALGY	GALLEY	Where Curry prepared lentil soup
SCSKA	CASKS	Wooden kegs to hold water
RAST	STAR	Slave woman Jessie thinks about
BUAC	CUBA	Where slaves are sold

VOCABULARY RESOURCE MATERIALS

VOCABULARY WORD SEARCH - *The Slave Dancer*

All the words in this list are associated with *The Slave Dancer* with emphasis on the vocabulary words being studied in the unit. The words are placed backwards, forward, diagonally, up and down. The included words are listed below the word search.

```
R E V I V I F I E D E I F I N G I D N U T G Y G
B E T J C A T T E N W C M E L M E P I N Z N J P
R X L D D I R G V S T P V A P K J D E C I H L V
S V L D R A G I B R A I T E C M P M E R N I V C
C Q L P N O S D A S T R N I M G A L B F G A A R
C E L Q L A E W S A O E M S N M X R U H I P R F
S U U F G V H I R M T I S I R Z P A T M T E Y J
C I R E A T V C O R M U D A W R L C P I B J D X
L K D R A E U R A F O N E J O O D B O O A D Y D
T L P K L L E B S R U R E F O E F U R Q E L E X
B E U Y L I L U O O U T U F M D S R B T D S R V
D R R M C E O U F C T S N I E R A L N Q S C Z D
S N O O I L G N S I I E R L Y H O E Q U S D E X
M Z B C I N O B S O S G A L S F M M R O I F D S
B A R R A C O O N S E P R O T E S T A T I O N S
C N E L F D N U S B M U R Y D F K H E L L X H K
Z P V I L E E S S I S M Q Y V L C F E K C A R W
```

ADDLES	CONFOUNDING	LAMENT	PROTESTATIONS
ALOOFNESS	CULPRIT	LANGUOROUS	RANCID
ARMAMENT	DEFIED	LOFTY	REVIVIFIED
ATHWART	DEFILE	LUCRATIVE	SPRY
BARRACOON	DEMENTED	LUMINOUS	SURLY
BEGRIMED	DEPRAVED	MARTIAL	TRANQUIL
BRINY	ENVISAGED	MIMICKED	TRUSSED
BROCADE	FETID	MORTAL	UNDIGNIFIED
CABOCIERO	FLOGGED	OBSCURE	VILE
CAPTIOUS	IMPALED	PERILOUS	WRACK
CHANDLER	IMPASSIVELY	PLIGHT	
CHAOS	IMPENETRABLE	PLUMB	
CLAMOR	JETTISON	PROFUSION	

VOCABULARY CROSSWORD - *The Slave Dancer*

VOCABULARY CROSSWORD CLUES - *The Slave Dancer*

ACROSS

3. Excess
8. Elaborate woven fabric with a raised design
10. Claudius and Purvis dumped Jessie on this
11. Black boy who survives with Jessie
12. Definite article
13. Confusion; disorder
14. Ship's cook
15. Opposite of 'follow'
16. Louisianian of French ancestry
17. Place where slaves will be sold
20. Supported
23. Possess
25. Faster than to walk; to —
26. Carpet
27. Pleasantly
30. Absolute; exact
32. Frozen water
34. Christian ship carpenter
36. Profitable
37. Cat's __; Purvis & Mary played this with Jessie
39. Ingest food
40. Fenced in
42. Crosswise; at right angles to the ship's keel
43. Tasteless

DOWN

1. Noble
2. Wail; sob
3. Dangerous
4. Foul
5. Limber; agile
6. Unknown; unfamiliar
7. Tied up
8. Enclosure of slaves
9. Uproar
14. Patrols U.S. shores; U.S. Revenue __
18. __ Stout; took Spark's place
19. Beheading
20. Testy
21. Roaring; blustery
22. Brilliant
24. Wretched; foul
28. Salty
29. Rotten
31. Guilty party
33. Used to try to clear stench from the hold; chloride of __
35. Opposite of 'alive'
38. Auditory organ
41. When there is no more, you've reached the __

VOCABULARY CROSSWORD - *The Slave Dancer*

166

VOCABULARY WORKSHEET 1 - *The Slave Dancer*

____ 1. Demented   A. Pictured

____ 2. Jettison   B. Control; restriction

____ 3. Envisage   C. Crazy; mad

____ 4. Impertinent   D. Excess

____ 5. Confounding   E. Glowing; radiant

____ 6. Undeterred   F. Shuffling

____ 7. Obscure   G. Puzzling; flustering

____ 8. Barbarousness   H. Dangerous

____ 9. Armament   I. Shamed; embarrassed

____ 10. Luminous   J. Dense; thick

____ 11. Shambling   K. Sassy; fresh

____ 12. Languorous   L. Horribly cruel

____ 13. Restraint   M. Arms; weapons

____ 14. Impenetrable   N. Profitable

____ 15. Profusion   O. Unknown; unfamiliar

____ 16. Perilous   P. Tied up

____ 17. Mortified   Q. Sleepy; lazy

____ 18. Lucrative   R. Abandon; get rid of

____ 19. Trussed   S. Unstopped

____ 20. Fetid   T. Foul

KEY: VOCABULARY WORKSHEET 1 - *The Slave Dancer*

__C__ 1. Demented		A. Pictured
__R__ 2. Jettison		B. Control; restriction
__A__ 3. Envisage		C. Crazy; mad
__K__ 4. Impertinent		D. Excess
__G__ 5. Confounding		E. Glowing; radiant
__S__ 6. Undeterred		F. Shuffling
__O__ 7. Obscure		G. Puzzling; flustering
__L__ 8. Barbarousness		H. Dangerous
__M__ 9. Armament		I. Shamed; embarrassed
__E__ 10. Luminous		J. Dense; thick
__F__ 11. Shambling		K. Sassy; fresh
__Q__ 12. Languorous		L. Horribly cruel
__B__ 13. Restraint		M. Arms; weapons
__J__ 14. Impenetrable		N. Profitable
__D__ 15. Profusion		O. Unknown; unfamiliar
__H__ 16. Perilous		P. Tied up
__I__ 17. Mortified		Q. Sleepy; lazy
__N__ 18. Lucrative		R. Abandon; get rid of
__P__ 19. Trussed		S. Unstopped
__T__ 20. Fetid		T. Foul

VOCABULARY WORKSHEET 2 - *The Slave Dancer*

___ 1. Flogged
___ 2. Holystoned
___ 3. Impenetrable
___ 4. Impassively
___ 5. Lament
___ 6. Ludicrous
___ 7. Keening
___ 8. Languorous
___ 9. Lucrative
___ 10. Ingenious
___ 11. Indistinct
___ 12. Doldrums
___ 13. Martial
___ 14. Convulsion
___ 15. Wrack
___ 16. Relinquish
___ 17. Pensively
___ 18. Placidly
___ 19. Rancid
___ 20. Mutinies

A. Unemotionally
B. Ridiculous
C. Wail; sob
D. Sleepy; lazy
E. Lashed; whipped
F. Profitable
G. Scrubbed clean with a soft sandstone
H. Unclear
I. Dense; thick
J. Mourning; wailing
K. Region of calm winds near the equator
L. Revolts; uprisings
M. Brilliant
N. Contraction; shaking
O. Military; warlike
P. Seaweed
Q. Thoughtfully
R. Rotten; foul
S. Give up
T. Peacefully

KEY: VOCABULARY WORKSHEET 2 - *The Slave Dancer*

_E_ 1. Flogged	A. Unemotionally
_G_ 2. Holystoned	B. Ridiculous
_I_ 3. Impenetrable	C. Wail; sob
_A_ 4. Impassively	D. Sleepy; lazy
_C_ 5. Lament	E. Lashed; whipped
_B_ 6. Ludicrous	F. Profitable
_J_ 7. Keening	G. Scrubbed clean with a soft sandstone
_D_ 8. Languorous	H. Unclear
_F_ 9. Lucrative	I. Dense; thick
_M_ 10. Ingenious	J. Mourning; wailing
_H_ 11. Indistinct	K. Region of calm winds near the equator
_K_ 12. Doldrums	L. Revolts; uprisings
_O_ 13. Martial	M. Brilliant
_N_ 14. Convulsion	N. Contraction; shaking
_P_ 15. Wrack	O. Military; warlike
_S_ 16. Relinquish	P. Seaweed
_Q_ 17. Pensively	Q. Thoughtfully
_T_ 18. Placidly	R. Rotten; foul
_R_ 19. Rancid	S. Give up
_L_ 20. Mutinies	T. Peacefully

JUGGLE LETTER VOCABULARY REVIEW GAME CLUES - *The Slave Dancer*

SCRAMBLED	WORD	CLUE
SHCAO	CHAOS	Confusion; disorder
DRAINECH	CHAGRINED	Annoyed
STIPUCAO	CAPTIOUS	Faultfinding
YLRSU	SURLY	Testy
DREEMIBG	BEGRIMED	Grimy; filthy
TTAARHW	ATHWART	Crosswise; at right angles with keel
GUAASES	ASSUAGE	Ease; relieve
MMAAENRT	ARMAMENT	Arms; weapons
CRAEOPHYT	APOTHECARY	Druggist; pharmacist
YBAAMLI	AMIABLY	Pleasantly
SOFALESON	ALOOFNESS	Indifference
DRIVEEGAG	AGGRIEVED	Pained
FTNCOFIILA	AFFLICTION	Disease
SLEDAD	ADDLES	Confuses
LOARMC	CLAMOR	Uproar
SEADDEB	DEBASED	Dishonorable
TREEBUMCCN	RECUMBENT	Leaning; idle
OONRPSUFI	PROFUSION	Excess
GLIPHT	PLIGHT	Sorry situation
XEEDPPRREL	PERPLEXED	Puzzled
SEENGIVA	ENVISAGE	Pictured
DEITD	FETID	Foul
GROWHARIN	HARROWING	Frightening
DEPALIM	IMPALED	Fenced in
NNMIITTREP	IMPERTINENT	Sassy; fresh
UNNIISOEG	INGENIOUS	Brilliant
TEJTSION	JETTISON	Abandon; get rid of
EMANT	LAMENT	Wail; sob
TYOLF	LOFTY	Noble

www.ingramcontent.com/pod-product-compliance
Lightning Source LLC
Chambersburg PA
CBHW051408070526
44584CB00023B/3337